CW00485187

Recipes For All Levels

Don't forget to join us on Facebook - https://www.facebook.com/groups/579682705929259

Introduction

We came together after running our Facebook group and formed an amazing friendship - total strangers running a group and then writing a book, all just adding what we could, no expectations, helping each other along with our strengths and weaknesses, and learning from each other along the way.

We all have completely different lives, but one thing we definitely all have in common is a love of food and air fryers, along with some other amazing kitchen gadgets. So, allow us to welcome you also into our little family and share our passion and inspiration to gain the most from your Dream Machine.

We have a varied range of things to try, using many different functions and even some store-cupboard staples to help with learning how to do things the Ninja® way. Our book is written to be function led rather than Ninja® model led and so covers a range of machines.

The Dream Team:

Dawn Keenan   Sonia Brundell   Bill Kingdon   Asha Joshi   Amy Leggat

Table To Help with Prep Time:

Look out for the below table showing timings, servings and if the recipe is for vegetarian or gluten free. This will be displayed on every page for your assistance.

Prep Time and Cook Time is shown as 'hrs' for hour(s) and 'm' for minute(s).

Prep Time -	Cook Time -	Serves -	Vegetarian ✔️	Vegan ✔️	Gluten Free ✔️

CONTENTS

Jargon Buster

AC	Air Crisp (same as Air Fry)
AF	Air-Fry (same as Air Crisp)
BROIL	Grill (if following an American recipe)
B/R	Bake/Roast
DEGLAZE	Ensuring the bottom of the main pot is scraped clear of anything that may be stuck to it before using the PC function – it avoids the 'ADD WATER' message
FMNT	Ferment for yoghurt making on models with the yoghurt function
PC	Pressure Cook
PIP	Pot-in-Pot
QR	Quick Release (moving from SEAL to VENT immediately after PC has completed)
NR	Natural Release (allowing the machine to slowly release pressure after PC whilst still In SEAL mode, the keep warm light comes on and the timer starts)
NPR	Natural Pressure release (same as NR)
SAUTE	Just as you would use a pan on the hob
SC	Slow Cook (you can use a glass lid that fits or the pressure lid on VENT. It is advisable to Saute on HI first to bring the pot up to heat before switching to SC)
STEAM	Set the valve set to VENT on the lid when using this function
STEAMB	Steam Bake
TRIVET	The low rack, or the holder for the air frying basket on Foodi models

Model Codes

OP100	Mini Foodi 4.5L (no grill, dehydrate or yoghurt function)
OP300	Medium Foodi 6L (no dehydrate or yoghurt function)
OP350	Medium Foodi (same functions as Foodi Max but 6L)
OP450	Same capacity as Foodi Max (no dehydrate or yoghurt function)
OP500	Foodi Max 7.5L (has dehydrate and yoghurt function)
OL550UK	6L 11-in-1 Foodi with Smart-Lid
OL650UK	7.5L 14-in-1 Foodi with Smart-Lid
OL750UK	7.5L 15-in-1 Foodi with Smart-Lid
SP101UK	Mini flip-oven 8-in-1
DT200UK	XL Oven with 10-in-1
AG301UK	Older grill model (deeper tray)
AG551UK	Newer grill model with probe (shallow tray but more cooking surface)
AG651UK	Newest grill model with more depth for cooking and flat Plate
AF300UK	Dual-zone air fryer
AF400UK	Max dual-zone air fryer

Useful Information

Foodi Max (OP500UK) **Air-Frying Basket Layering-Up Hack**

If you are the owner of a *Foodi Max – OP500UK* model this is a great hack for multi-layer cooking when using the air frying basket – a good old-fashioned chip mesh! *(See photo)*. Dimensions are 8" width and 3" depth available in hardware shops or on the internet. Once the handles are removed, this mesh sits nicely in the *Foodi Max OP500* air frying basket for an extra layer to do chips on the top and meat stuff at the bottom in one hit!

Baking in Silicone Without a 'Bake Belly'

Often, when baking in silicone loaf moulds, cakes and bakes are prone to get a bulge in the middle, which isn't always aesthetically pleasing.

To help keep the shape, foil batons can be made to fit and hold the sides of the mould in place whilst cooking, by securing them between the mould and the main pot of the gadget that is being used.

Note: Some adjustment to the foils will be required whilst cooking and it must be remembered that the foil is hot so care must be taken

In the spirit of recycling, foil batons may be retained to be used again.

Maximising Space When Baking by Using Pleated Paper Cases or Silicone Moulds

Whilst, as a rule, anything that has been used in an oven may be used in a Ninja® gadget, what we may already have may not always fit. And so, we are prompted to buy new accessories to use which can sometimes be expensive and are not always practical to maximise the available cooking space. Pleated paper muffin cases or silicone moulds *(see photos)* are a great way to "pile 'em in" and cook cupcakes, muffins or even steamed eggs!

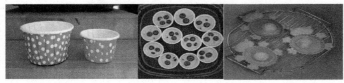

Conversion Tables

CONVERSION TABLES/CHARTS

WEIGHT

IMPERIAL	METRIC
½oz	15g
1oz	29g
2oz	57g
3oz	85g
4oz	113g
5oz	141g
6oz	170g
8oz	227g
10oz	283g
12oz	340g
13oz	369g
14oz	397g
15oz	425g
1lb	453g

TEMPERATURE

FAHRENHEIT	CELCIUS
100°F	37°C
150°F	65°C
200°F	93°C
250°F	121°C
300°F	150°C
325°F	160°C
350°F	180°C
375°F	190°C
400°F	200°C
425°F	220°C
450°F	230°C
500°F	260°C
525°F	274°C
550°F	288°C

ROUND CAKE TIN/LID SIZES

CM	INCHES
15cm	6in
20cm	8in
23cm	9in
25cm	10in

MEASUREMENTS

CUP	OUNCES	MILLILITRES	TABLESPOONS
1/16 cup	½oz	15ml	1 tbsp
⅛ cup	1oz	30ml	3 tbsp
¼ cup	2oz	59ml	4 tbsp
⅓ cup	2.5oz	79ml	5.5 tbsp
⅜ cup	3oz	90ml	6 tbsp
½ cup	4oz	118ml	8 tbsp
⅔ cup	5oz	158ml	11 tbsp
¾ cup	6oz	177ml	12 tbsp
1 cup	8oz	240ml	16 tbsp
2 cup	16oz	480ml	32 tbsp
4 cup	32oz	960ml	64 tbsp
5 cup	40oz	1180ml	80 tbsp
6 cup	48oz	1420ml	96 tbsp
8 cup	64oz	1895ml	128 tbsp

SPOONS

SPOON SIZE	ML
tsp	5ml
dspn	10ml
tbsp	15ml

MISCELLANEOUS MEASUREMENTS

HELPFUL GUIDANCE CHART - OLD SCHOOL STYLE	
1 dash	6 drops
1 pinch	1/16 tsp
1 stick of butter	¼lb/113 g
1lb sugar	2¼ cups
1lb flour	3⅓ cups

AIR FRYER CONVERSION CHART

OVEN TIME	AIR FRYER
10 Minutes	8 Minutes
15 Minutes	12 Minutes
20 Minutes	16 Minutes
25 Minutes	20 Minutes
30 Minutes	24 Minutes
35 Minutes	28 Minutes
40 Minutes	32 Minutes
45 Minutes	36 Minutes
50 Minutes	40 Minutes
55 Minutes	44 Minutes
60 Minutes	48 Minutes

OVEN	OVEN FAN	AIR FRYER
190C	170C	150C
200C	180C	160C
210C	190C	170C
220C	200C	180C
230C	210C	190C

Sides/Accompaniments

HEALTHY MASH POTATO - LOW CARB (BATCH COOKED)

Prep Time - 10m	Cook Time - 10m	Serves - 6/8	Vegan ✔	Gluten Free✔

INGREDIENTS

3 medium white potatoes (quartered)
2 large, sweet potatoes cut into same size as white potato
2 carrots (thinly sliced)
1 swede (diced)
Salt to taste
¼ to ½ bag of spinach (finely chopped)
2 cups of cold water

Tips/Variations (optional):

To cook after freezing, defrost overnight, then add to a small oven dish. Cook on AIR FRY set at 200 degrees for 8 minutes, stirring a couple of times.
Butter and milk may be added at Step 3

Difficulty: Easy

Ninja® Functions: PRESSURE COOK, AIR FRY

Freezable: Yes (see Tips/Variations)

DIRECTIONS

1. Place the water and all ingredients except the salt and the spinach into the main pot.
2. PRESSURE COOK ON HI for 5 minutes followed by QUICK RELEASE.
3. Empty out most of the water, leaving a little in the pot so it's wet at the bottom.
4. Add the spinach and mash it all in.
5. Once mashed, salt to taste.
6. This is great used as a topping for a shepherd's pie or served with sausages.

SPICY PANEER 'CHIPS'

Prep Time - 5m	Cook Time - 7m	Serves - 2	Vegetarian ✓

INGREDIENTS

1 slab of shop-bought paneer
Shan® vegetable masala seasoning or
any dry seasoning of your choice
1 fresh lemon wedge (juice only)

Tips/Variations (optional):
Paneer is a versatile, hard, Indian cheese.
Both these items ought to be available in
the world food chilled and store cupboard
sections in major, well-known
supermarkets, or in Indian grocery stores.

Difficulty: Easy
Ninja® Functions: AIR FRY
Freezable: Yes

DIRECTIONS

1. Cut the paneer slab into 'chips', approx. 1cm x 6cm. Place the 'chipped' paneer into a plastic food bag or a lidded food container and sprinkle over the vegetable masala or seasoning of your choice.
2. Give the bag or food container a good shake to coat each chip with the seasoning.
3. Place the air frying basket into the machine and select the AIR FRY function set to 180 degrees to preheat for 3 minutes, or until the 'ADD FOOD' notification appears.
4. Spread the 'chipped' paneer out in the basket and cook for 7 minutes, moving around 2 or 3 times during cooking.
5. Once cooked, place paneer chips on a serving plate and squeeze the lemon juice over them.
6. Serve with yoghurt and mint dip and enjoy!

SAAG ALOO

Prep Time - 10m	Cook Time - 6/8m	Serves - ¾	Vegan ✔	Gluten Free ✔

INGREDIENTS
4 medium-sized potatoes
¼ of a bag of spinach
1 onion
½ tiny diced red bell pepper
4 tbsp olive oil
1 tsp mustard seeds
1 tsp cumin seeds
½ tsp coriander powder
½ tsp turmeric
2 garlic cloves
1 tsp easy red chilli
1 tbsp ginger paste
1 tomato, chopped
100ml water
Salt to taste

GF – Please check spices for 'may contain' ingredient advisories.

Difficulty: Easy
Ninja® Functions: PRESSURE COOK, SAUTE
Freezable: Yes

DIRECTIONS
1. Add water to the main pot, filling to the 2 cups marker.
2. Chop the potatoes into small cubes, put directly into the water and PRESSURE COOK on LOW for 2 minutes, QUICK RELEASE.
3. Empty out the water and set aside the potatoes.
4. Add the oil to the pot and SAUTE on MEDIUM heat, add the mustard seeds, cumin seeds, garlic, and ginger paste.
5. Cook for a few minutes until the spices are popping.
6. Add the diced onion, chopped tomato, red chilli, turmeric, coriander powder and red pepper. SAUTE until the onions are soft and the mixture is cooked and mixed nicely. Add the potatoes and SAUTE stirring the mixture.
7. Add the spinach and water, cook until the spinach has wilted - should be just a minute or two.
8. Add salt to taste and serve.

HASSELBACK POTATOES

Prep Time - 12m	Cook Time - 20/30m	Serves - 3	Gluten Free✔□

INGREDIENTS

12 very small potatoes
½ tsp cracked black pepper
Handful of grated cheese
12 pepperoni slices cut into quarters
4 ham slices cut into squares
1 sliced onion

Difficulty: Easy
Ninja® Functions: AIR FRY
Freezable: No

DIRECTIONS

1. Slice almost through the potatoes, leaving about 1cm unsliced all the way along.
2. Then select the AIR FRY setting at 180 degrees and cook for about 20-25 minutes (until the potatoes are soft).
3. Carefully place slices of pepperoni, cheese, ham and onions in each groove until the potatoes are fully loaded.
4. AIR FRY for a further 8-10 minutes at 180 degrees.

MASHED POTATOES

Prep Time - 8/12m	Cook Time - 5m	Serves - 4	Vegetarian v/0	Gluten Free✔

INGREDIENTS
4 medium potatoes (peeled and quartered)
2 tbsp butter
½ tsp salt
¼ pint milk
2 cups of cold water

Difficulty: Easy
Ninja® Functions: PRESSURE COOK
Freezable: Yes

DIRECTIONS

1. Add 2 cups of water to the pot.
2. Peel and cut the potatoes into quarters.
3. PRESSURE COOK on HI for 5 minutes, followed by QUICK RELEASE.
4. Empty out the water, add the butter and salt and mash.
5. Pour enough milk in and stir to achieve the desired consistency.

SALTED ROAST POTATOES

Prep Time - 10m	Cook Time - 40m	Serves - 4	Vegan ✔	Gluten Free ✔

INGREDIENTS
4 large potatoes (peeled and quartered)
1 tbsp oil
Pinch of salt
Tips / Variations (optional):
You can also sprinkle a stock cube over them to give them a real full flavour - dried sage and onion stuffing mix also works really well!

Difficulty: Easy
Ninja® Functions: PRESSURE COOK, AIR FRY
Freezable: Yes

DIRECTIONS

1. Peel and cut the potatoes into quarters. Add them to the pot and fill with water to the 2 cups mark. PRESSURE COOK on HI for 4 minutes followed by QUICK RELEASE.
2. Empty out the water, put the potatoes into a bowl and spray them with vegetable oil and add a little salt, stir to coat the potatoes.
3. Place into the air frying basket and AIR FRY at 180 degrees for 25 minutes, turning them halfway.

CHIPS - SALT, PEPPER AND CHILLI FLAVOURED

Prep Time - 12m	Cook Time - 23/30m	Serves - 4	Vegan ✔	Gluten Free ✔

INGREDIENTS

4 medium potatoes
1-2 tbsp oil
Pinch of salt and black pepper
½ thinly sliced/chopped chilli (depending on how hot you like them)
Fresh parsley to top

Tips / Variations (optional):

You can add some finely grated cheese or for plain chips, follow the instructions above and leave out the chilli powder, pepper and salt if desired.

Difficulty: Easy
Ninja® Functions: AIR FRY
Freezable: Yes

DIRECTIONS

1. Peel and 'chip' the potatoes then wash them in cold water until the water runs clear.
2. Pat the chips dry with a clean tea towel, then add them to a large bowl and pour over the oil, salt, black pepper and chilli.
3. Stir thoroughly with a wooden spoon until the chips are completely coated in oil.
4. Add to the air frying basket and AIR FRY at 180 degrees for 25 minutes, stirring them a couple of times.
5. Top with the parsley and serve.

POTATO WEDGES

Prep Time - 8/10m	Cook Time - 18m	Serves - 2	Vegan ✔	Gluten Free ✔

INGREDIENTS
4 medium-sized potatoes with skin on
Olive oil (sprayed or brushed-on with a pastry brush)
Chilli flakes (optional, or a seasoning of your choice)
Tips / Variations (optional):
Floury potatoes like Maris Pipers are recommended.

Difficulty: Easy
Ninja® Functions: AIR FRY
Freezable: Yes

DIRECTIONS

1. Cut the potatoes into wedges and soak in cold water for 30 minutes.
2. Pat dry, oil and season with chilli flakes or a seasoning of your choice (optional).
3. Select the AIR FRY function and preheat to 180 degrees. Place the air frying basket in the main pot to also preheat.
4. Place wedges directly into the air frying basket and cook at 180 degrees for 15 minutes with periodic moving around.
5. Ramp the temperature up to 200 degrees and cook for a further 3 minutes with periodic moving around.

GLUTEN FREE - POTATO PANCAKES

Prep Time - 15m	Cook Time - 15m	Serves - 2/4	Vegetarian ✔	Gluten free ✔

INGREDIENTS

300g of left-over mashed potato
½ tsp baking powder
100g gluten-free plain flour
Note: This will vary depending on how buttery your mash was - start with half this amount of flour and just keep adding until it comes together into a Play-Doh®-like texture.

Difficulty: Easy/Medium
Ninja® Functions: SAUTE
Freezable: Yes

DIRECTIONS

1. In a bowl, mix together the mash, baking powder and flour to form a ball. Add the flour gradually so it doesn't end up too dry.
2. Roll into a sausage shape and cut into 8 equal pieces.
3. On a floured surface roll out each piece into a small circle, approximately ½cm thick.
4. Select the SAUTE function set on HI to heat up for 3 minutes. Add the potato cakes in and dry fry them for 3-4 minutes on each side or until browned nicely.
5. Smother with butter and enjoy.

POMME NOISETTES

Prep Time - 15/20m	Cook Time - 8m	Serves - 4	Vegetarian ✔	Gluten Free ✔

INGREDIENTS

Mashed potato (as per 'Mashed Potato' recipe in Sides/Accompaniments)

Tips/Variations (optional):
For a healthier mash, an egg may be cracked into the potatoes immediately after PRESSURE COOK and mashed and mixed in.

If making these in the Ninja® Grill model, they may be piped directly into the main pot once it has been oiled to maximise the quantity that may be cooked at any one time.

Difficulty: Easy
Ninja® Functions: PRESSURE COOK, AIR FRY
Freezable: Yes

DIRECTIONS

1. Place mashed potato into a piping bag with a star nozzle and pipe into an oiled baking tin to form noisettes.
2. Select the AIR FRY function and set at 200 degrees and preheat for 3 minutes.
3. Place the baking tin directly into the main pot and cook for 8 minutes.

ROAST POTATOES - 3 NINJA® FUNCTION

Prep Time - 8/10m	Cook Time - 30m	Serves - 3 to 4	Vegan ✔	Gluten Free ✔

INGREDIENTS
3-4 medium-sized potatoes (peeled and quartered)
250ml cold water
Rapeseed oil (spray)
Tips/Variations (optional):
If your machine does not have the PRESSURE COOK function, this may be completed by par-boiling the potatoes in a pan on the hob. Floury potatoes like Maris Pipers are recommended.

Difficulty: Medium
Ninja® Functions: PRESSURE COOK, ROAST, AIR FRY
Freezable: Yes (after ROAST step. Then reheat from frozen using AIR FRY function at 180 degrees for 15-20 minutes)

DIRECTIONS

1. Pour 250ml cold water into the main pot and insert the air frying basket. Place the potatoes into the basket, select the PRESSURE COOK function and set to HI, set the timer to 2 minutes start. Once this completes, move the dial to the VENT position and QUICK RELEASE. Once complete, remove the basket from the machine.

2. Give the potatoes a good shake whilst in the basket to rough up the edges – remember, the basket will be hot so use oven gloves to hold it. It is advisable to complete this step over the sink as some of the potato will fly out of the holes of the basket. Empty out the water from the main pot.

3. Remove the potatoes from the basket onto a plate and leave to go cold – this is optional, but it is helpful if you are using one machine to cook your whole meal. When the potatoes are ready to be cooked, select the ROAST function on the machine and set at 170 degrees and preheat for 3 minutes, or until the 'ADD FOOD' notification appears.

4. In the meantime, spray the potatoes with rapeseed oil to evenly coat them and then place in the air frying basket and cook for 15 minutes, moving them around periodically using tongs. More oil may be sprayed over the potatoes if desired to ensure they don't look dried out (optional). Switch to AIR FRY function and set at 200 degrees and cook the potatoes for a further 5 minutes.

ROASTED VEG MEDLEY

Prep Time - 15/20m	Cook Time - 25m	Serves - 4	Vegan ✔☐	Gluten Free✔☐

INGREDIENTS

4 medium potatoes (peeled and quartered)
2 parsnips (peeled and cut into 5cm long batons)
5 tendersweet carrots (peeled and halved)
2 small red onions (peeled and quartered)
Rapeseed oil (spray)
1 teaspoon dried rosemary

Tips/Variations (optional):
Floury potatoes are recommended. The core of parsnips can be 'woody' in which case it is recommended to remove them.

Difficulty: Easy
Ninja® Functions: ROAST, AIR FRY
Freezable: Yes

DIRECTIONS

1. Chop the potatoes and leave to soak in cold water for 30 minutes. Pat the potatoes dry and place in a lidded food container and spray with rapeseed oil to coat and sprinkle in the dried rosemary. Give the container a good shake to distribute the oil and dried rosemary evenly.

2. Place the air frying basket into the machine and select the ROAST function the set to 180 degrees and preheat for 3 minutes.

3. Add in the potatoes and cook for 10 minutes with periodic moving around using tongs. In the meantime, place the parsnips and carrots into the lidded food container, spray with rapeseed oil and give the container a shake to distribute the oil evenly over the veg.

4. Add the carrots and parsnips to the air frying basket along with the potatoes and cook for 5 minutes, moving around periodically. In the meantime, place the red onion into the lidded container and spray with oil and shake the container to distribute the oil evenly.

5. Add the onions to the air frying basket along with the other veg and cook for 5 minutes with periodic moving around. Switch to AIR FRY function set at 200 degrees and continue to cook the veg for a further 5 minutes.

6. Serve as a side with roast dinner or a pie and enjoy!

AIR FRY BREAD

Prep Time - 2 hrs 10m	Cook Time - 20m	Serves - 3/4	Vegetarian

INGREDIENTS
500g strong white bread flour
7g sachet fast-action yeast
2 tsp salt
2 tbsp olive oil
300ml water

Difficulty: Easy/Medium
Ninja® Functions: DEHYDRATE, AIR FRY
Freezable: Yes

DIRECTIONS

1. Mix together the flour, salt and yeast. Make a well in the centre of the mixture and add the oil and water and then mix it in to form a dough and knead for 10 minutes. Mould the mixture together into a ball.
2. Oil a cake tin and place the dough in, rubbing some oil over the dough. Cover with a damp cloth or some cling film.
3. Prove the dough for 1 hour and 50 minutes using the DEHYDRATE function at 40 degrees or at room temperature, until the dough has doubled in size.
4. Shape the dough into a loaf and then pre-heat the machine using AIR FRY function set at 200 degrees for a few minutes. Add the dough in the tin to the machine using the low rack and AIR FRY for 20 minutes.
5. Allow the bread to cool for 30 minutes before cutting and serving.

STEAMBAKE BREAD

Prep Time - 1 hrs 45m	Cook Time - 10m	Serves - 7	Vegetarian ✓

INGREDIENTS
500g plain flour
1¼ tsp salt
3 tbsp sugar
2 tbsp butter
1 tbsp yeast
250ml warm milk
60ml warm water
A little oil for greasing

Difficulty: Easy/Medium
Ninja® Functions: SAUTE, PROVE, STEAMBAKE
Freezable: Yes

DIRECTIONS

1. Combine the water and milk in the main pot and SAUTE on medium heat until it starts to foam, then set aside for 10 minutes. Add the yeast, (the temp should be around 40 degrees).
2. Add the butter, flour, salt and sugar and knead together by hand for 10 minutes or use the knead setting if you have the processor (you can also use a whisk). Add a little oil to the dough ball and prove for 50 minutes at 35°C.
3. Push the dough down and split it to make 7 balls of dough.
4. Add 250ml of water to the main pot, place the dough balls in the air frying basket in a circle with one in the middle as in the above photo and prove for 30 minutes at 35 degrees.
5. Select the STEAM BAKE function set at 160 degrees and bake for 10 minutes.

Light Bites/Lunches

CHEESE ON TOAST - MADE SPECIAL!

Prep Time - 5m	Cook Time - 5m	Serves - 1 per slice

INGREDIENTS
1 slice of bread per person
Sliced cheese
Fillings:
1 mushroom, for 2 slices
2 slices of chorizo, diced
A sprinkle of black cracked pepper
A sprinkle of parsley or chives

Tips/Variations (optional):
You can also use:
Thin slices of onion
Tiny bits of pre-cooked bacon and/or sausage
Ham
Finely diced peppers/bell peppers
Salami
Olives
Pineapple

Difficulty: Easy
Ninja® Functions: AIR FRY
Freezable: No

DIRECTIONS

1. Place the bread slices on a board, chop any toppings of your choice - Meats, unless they are wafer-thin, will need to be pre-cooked and place on the bread.
2. Add the cheese followed by the sliced/diced toppings. More cheese may be added later if desired.
3. AIR FRY at 240 degrees for 5 minutes with no preheat, or until the cheese is melted and bubbling to your preference.

GLUTEN FREE HAM, CHEESE AND RED ONION TOASTIE

Prep Time - 5m	Cook Time - 5/6m	Serves - 1	Gluten Free✔

INGREDIENTS

Cheese (as preferred)
Ham
Red onion
Butter
Dijon mustard
3 slices of gluten-free bread (Warburtons®
gluten free toastie bread is recommended)

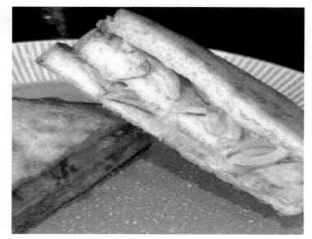

Difficulty: Easy
Ninja® Functions: GRILL
Freezable: No

DIRECTIONS

1. Set the GRILL function to MEDIUM setting with the air frying basket in place).

2. Add one of the slices of bread during the preheating stage (this will be the middle piece) and grill until slightly browned, flipping over so both sides are done. This will take a few minutes, keeping a check periodically to ensure it is not over done. Take out and set aside.

3. Butter one side of the slices of bread then start to assemble the toastie.

4. Butter side down first, then cheese, red onion, then ham.

5. Spread the Dijon mustard on both sides of the toasted piece and add that on top, then more ham, onion, then cheese and the last piece of bread, butter side up.

6. Once the machine comes up with the 'ADD FOOD' notification, place the toastie into the air frying basket and GRILL for 4 minutes on MEDIUM. Flip it over, turn down to LOW and toast for a further 4 minutes.

7. How thick you slice your cheese will depend on how quickly it will melt, so just cut it in half once the time is up and if it's not oozing then just simply put it back in for a few more minutes, checking regularly.

TANDOORI CHICKEN FILLETS

Prep Time - 10/15m (4 hrs marinating)	Cook Time - 20m	Serves - 2	Gluten free✔

INGREDIENTS

500g mini chicken fillets
1 large lemon (juice only)
250ml buttermilk
2 tbsp tandoori powder/masala
2-3 green chillies (chopped)
A handful of chopped fresh coriander

Tips/Variations (optional):
Natural yoghurt may be used as an
alternative to buttermilk.

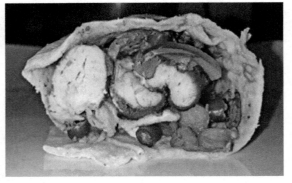

Difficulty: Easy
Ninja® Functions: ROAST, GRILL
Freezable: No

DIRECTIONS

1. Place the chicken in a large bowl and fork all over to create holes in the chicken. Cut the lemon in half and squeeze the juice over the chicken and stir – retain the other lemon half in reserve.

2. Pour in the buttermilk, and add the tandoori powder/masala, chopped chillies and chopped coriander to the chicken and give everything a stir to ensure it is covered with the tandoori marinade. Transfer the chicken to a lidded food container and sprinkle on some chopped coriander (optional) and leave to marinade in the fridge for 4 hours (overnight also works).

3. Select the ROAST function on the machine and set to 180 degrees and preheat for 3 minutes or until the 'ADD FOOD' notification appears.

4. Place the chicken into an ovenproof dish and place it on the low rack and cook for 10 minutes turning over halfway. Retain the leftover marinade to 'top up' on the chicken and use the reserve lemon to squeeze more lemon juice over the chicken during cooking.

5. Switch to GRILL function and continue to cook the chicken for a further 6 minutes turning halfway. This phase of cooking will give the chicken a chargrilled effect.

6. Serve in warmed gluten free wraps with salad and chilli and garlic sauce and enjoy!

MILK ROLL BRUSCHETTA

Prep Time - 8/10m	Cook Time - 4/5m	Serves - 2/4

INGREDIENTS

4 slices of milk roll bread
1½ tbsp butter (very soft)
½ tsp garlic granules
10 plum tomatoes (chopped into small pieces)
Salt and pepper (to season)
1 tsp (dried basil)
Olive oil (to drizzle)
3-4 tsp of grated parmigiano cheese

Difficulty: Easy
Ninja® Functions: ROAST, AIR FRY
Freezable: No

DIRECTIONS

1. Mix together the butter and the garlic granules in a small bowl to prepare the garlic butter and leave to one side.
2. Place the tomatoes, dried basil and parmigiano cheese in a bowl, season with salt and pepper and drizzle with the olive oil, then mix together with a spoon until the tomatoes are coated with the oil, cheese and seasonings to prepare the tomato topping.
3. Select the AIR FRY function and set to 180 degrees and preheat for 2 minutes or until the 'ADD FOOD' notification appears.
4. Meanwhile, spread the garlic butter over the milk roll. Place the bread directly onto either the main pot of the machine, or on wire racks if preferred, and cook for 1 minute.
5. Spoon and spread the tomato topping directly onto the milk roll whilst in the machine.
6. Select the ROAST function and set to 180 degrees and cook the bruschetta for 3 minutes.
7. Select the AIR FRY function and set to 180 degrees and cook for a further 1-2 minutes. Sprinkle with more parmigiano cheese (optional) before serving – this may be enjoyed as a tasty and easy starter or light lunch for a midweek meal.

INDIAN OMELETTE

| Prep Time - 8/10m | Cook Time - 13/15m | Serves - 2 | Vegetarian ✓ | Gluten free✔ |

INGREDIENTS
4 medium sized eggs (at room temperature)
1 medium onion (finely chopped)
1 finger chilli (sliced)
1 tsp ginger (grated)
1 tsp garam masala
½ tsp cooking salt
½ tsp chilli powder (optional)
Handful of coriander (leaves only, finely chopped)
Cooking oil (spray for baking tray only)

Tips/Variations (optional):
The same mixture may be used in a silicone muffin tray to make eggy bites.
GF – Please check spices for 'may contain' ingredient advisories.

Difficulty: Easy
Ninja® Functions: BAKE
Freezable: No

DIRECTIONS

1. Place all the ingredients (except the oil) into a mixing bowl and whisk together with a fork or hand whisk. This needs a bit of hard work to ensure all the ingredients are mixed together and the mixture has a frothy appearance.
2. Select the BAKE function and set to 170 degrees and preheat for 3 minutes or until the 'ADD FOOD' notification appears.
3. Meanwhile, spray an ovenproof dish with oil and pour the omelette mixture into it.
4. Place the dish into the main pot of the machine, either on a silicone mat or the low rack, and cook for 15 minutes – adjust time if needed to ensure the mixture is cooked through and firm to the touch.
5. Serve in bread with tomato ketchup and enjoy!

MARMITE® AND CHEESE CHICKEN MELTS

Prep Time - 8/10m	Cook Time - 20m	Serves - 2

INGREDIENTS
4 boneless and skinless chicken thighs
2 tsp Marmite®
100g grated cheese

Difficulty: Easy
Ninja® Functions: ROAST, AIR FRY
Freezable: No

DIRECTIONS

1. Apply ½ a teaspoon of Marmite® to each gashed chicken thigh and wrap in cling film. Placing the chicken between your hands, massage the Marmite® onto the thigh to evenly coat each.
2. Select the ROAST function on the machine and set to 180 degrees.
3. Remove chicken from cling film and place in an ovenproof tin and cook for 15 minutes.
4. Sprinkle with the grated cheese and switch to AIR FRY function set at 200 degrees and cook for a further 5 minutes until the cheese is brown and bubbly.
5. Serve with chips and buttered sweetcorn.

EGG BITES x10 CUPCAKE SIZE

Prep Time - 10m	Cook Time - 10m	Serves - 4

INGREDIENTS
4 eggs
50g cheese
50g garlic and herb roule
2 tbsp double cream
Fillings, I used:
1 onion (diced)
3 slices of ham
¼ red pepper

Difficulty: Easy/Medium
Ninja® Functions: STEAM
Freezable: No

DIRECTIONS

1. Pour 2 cups of water into the main pot of the machine.
2. Whizz together the eggs, add the diced onion, cheese, roule, cream, and any other diced fillings, do a short burst pulse to break up a little in a blender.
3. Fill the silicon cake cases almost to the top. Select the STEAM function and ensure the valve is set to VENT position and cook for 10 minutes.
4. If you only have one rack for the machine, these may be cooked in batches of 5.

ROASTED TOMATO SOUP

Prep Time - 12m	Cook Time - 20m	Serves - 4	Vegetarian ✔	Gluten free ✔

INGREDIENTS

9 fresh large tomatoes
1 large red onion
3 garlic cloves
1 tbsp of balsamic vinegar
1 tsp salt
1 tsp Black pepper
1 tbsp oil
2 tbsp tomato puree
1 tbsp brown sugar
1 tbsp dried basil
2 chicken (or vegetable stock cubes if vegetarian) GF ** - Can be adapted to Gluten Free by swapping the highlighted ingredients to GF.
700ml water

Difficulty: Easy/Medium
Ninja® Functions: BAKE, PRESSURE COOK, Soup Maker
Freezable: Yes

DIRECTIONS

1. Chop the tomatoes and onion into quarters and place into the main pot.
2. Add the garlic, balsamic vinegar, salt and pepper and drizzle over the oil. Select the BAKE function on the machine set at 200 degrees and cook for 10 minutes.
3. Once complete, add the puree, sugar, basil, stock cubes and water and PRESSURE COOK on HI for 5 minutes followed by NATURAL RELEASE for 5 minutes. Then QUICK RELEASE.
4. Blend and serve.
5. Add a little cream to the centre using a spoon if you wish.

STEAMED EGGS

Prep Time - 1m	Cook Time - 2m	Serves - 1	Vegetarian ✔	Gluten free✔

INGREDIENTS

Eggs
A little oil to grease the silicone moulds
2 cups cold water

Tips / Variations (optional):
A glass lid may be used. If using the
pressure-cooking lid, only steam for 1
minute with the vent open.
Sprinkle with parsley/black pepper and
served on toast.

Difficulty: Easy
Ninja® Functions: STEAM
Freezable: No

DIRECTIONS

1. Fill to the 2 cups level inside the pot with water, spray the moulds with a little oil and rub around to coat them.
2. Crack the eggs into the mould and place directly into the water - place them to the side of the bowl to stop them from tipping over.
3. Place the glass lid or Ninja lid on the top, and steam for 2 minutes, then serve immediately.

BACON-WRAPPED SCOTCH EGGS

Prep Time - 15m	Cook Time - 30/35m	Serves - 4	Gluten free ✔

INGREDIENTS

4 eggs
8 streaky bacon slices
2 packs of sausage meat GF ** - Can be adapted to Gluten Free by swapping the highlighted ingredients to GF.

Tips/Variations (optional):
You can alternatively roll in breadcrumbs GF ** - Can be adapted to Gluten Free by swapping the highlighted ingredients to GF for a normal scotch egg, or you can also add stuffing or cheese instead of the egg to the middle. Another nice addition is some cranberry sauce added to the bacon before folding in.

Difficulty: Easy
Ninja® Functions: PRESSURE COOK, AIR FRY
Freezable: Yes

DIRECTIONS

1. Add the eggs to a rack with 2 cups of water in the main pot and PRESSURE COOK on HI for 4 minutes, then QUICK RELEASE and put into a bowl of cold water.
2. Once cooled, peel the eggs, and set aside. Flatten out the sausage meat into patties using enough to wrap around each egg. Do this with all of them.
3. Place two pieces of streaky bacon in a cross shape, add the sausage wrapped eggs to the middle and wrap the bacon around, one bit at a time.
4. Parchment paper may be added to the air frying basket before placing the scotch eggs into it.
5. Select the AIR FRY function set at 200 degrees and cook for 20 to 25 minutes.

Main Dishes

CHINESE CHICKEN THIGHS

Prep Time - 8/10m	Cook Time - 25/30m	Serves - 1	Gluten free✔

INGREDIENTS
3 chicken thighs
Sesame seeds to top
For The Sauce: -
½ tbsp oil
4 tsp soy sauce GF ** - Can be adapted to Gluten Free by swapping the highlighted ingredients to GF.
4 tsp sweet chilli Sauce
½ tsp ginger and garlic paste
1 tsp light brown sugar
½ tsp apple cider vinegar

Difficulty: Easy/Medium
Ninja® Functions: PRESSURE COOK, AIR FRY
Freezable: No

DIRECTIONS

1. Mix all the sauce ingredients together.
2. Fill the po to the 2 cups mark with water in the main pot and place the chicken thighs in the air frying basket, and PRESSURE COOK on HI for 7 minutes followed by NATURAL RELEASE for 7 minutes, followed by QUICK RELEASE.
3. Empty the water out and place the thighs in an ovenproof dish on a low rack.
4. Switch to AIR FRY function set at 200 degrees and cook for another 12 minutes.
5. Use any leftover sauce in the ovenproof dish to pour over the chicken and top with the sesame seeds.

TURKEY BURGERS

Prep Time - 10m	Cook Time - 15m	Serves - 4

INGREDIENTS
800g turkey mince
2 slices brown bread (crumbed)
1 egg
1 red onion (finely diced)
1 tsp tomato paste
1 crushed garlic clove
1 tsp salt
1 tsp sage
1 tbsp fish sauce
2 tbsp ketchup

Difficulty: Easy
Ninja® Functions: AIR FRY or GRILL
Freezable: Yes (before or after cooking)

DIRECTIONS

1. With processor: crumb the bread in the processor, then add all the other ingredients and pulse or, using medium, dough until it's all chopped and mixed.
2. Chop the onion very small either by hand or in a food processor, crumb the bread, crack in the egg, then add all the other ingredients, and use your fingers to squash and mix until it's all mixed in and bound together.
3. Separate the ingredients into 8, roll each section into a ball, then flatten into a burger shaped patty, or use a burger shaper.
4. Select the AIR FRY function set at 200 degrees for 15 minutes, turning halfway.
5. Serve on salad or in a bread roll, and add melted cheese, tomato, lettuce if you desire.

BILL'S GREAT BEEF STIFADO - GREEK BEEF STEW

Prep Time - 3hrs 10m	Cook Time - 2 hrs 30m	Serves - 4	Gluten free✔

INGREDIENTS

For the marinade:

2-3 bay leaves

2 tsp-dried oregano

125ml red wine, plus some for yourself

2 tbsp red wine vinegar

3 garlic cloves, peeled and crushed

4 cloves

2 cinnamon sticks, broken into large pieces

For the beef:

750g-1kg diced beef

A good glug of good olive oil

500g shallots or small onions (peeled)

400g can of chopped tomatoes

2 tbsp tomato purée

Beef stock cubes or two stock pots GF ** - Can be adapted to Gluten Free by swapping the highlighted ingredients to GF.

200ml water

Difficulty: Medium

Ninja® Functions: SAUTE, PRESSURE COOK, SLOW COOK

Freezable: Yes

DIRECTIONS

1. Mix all the marinade ingredients in a large dish. Add beef and chill for 3 hours. Select the SAUTE function set and set to HI. Add some olive oil and once heated reduce to MEDIUM.

2. SAUTE the onions or shallots until just changing colour. Remove the beef from the marinade (keep marinade) and brown the beef on HI until a little brown.

3. Add the tomatoes and tomato puree and the reserved marinade to the main pot. It is important to thoroughly deglaze the pan at this point to prevent burning during pressure cooking.

4. Add water and stock.

5. PRESSURE COOK for 10 minutes, followed by NATURAL RELEASE for 10 minutes. Add onions and shallots and season to taste.

6. Switch to SAUTE and bring to a simmer.

7. Switch to SLOW COOK on LOW and leave for at least 2 hours, but the beef can withstand much more time.

8. Switch to SAUTE MEDIUM and bring to a simmer. I added a little corn flour slurry and mixed it in. Let the sauce thicken a little. Serve and enjoy.

BEEF BALTI

Prep Time - 20m	Cook Time - 30m or 3 hrs	Serves - 4	Gluten free✔☐

INGREDIENTS
700g diced beef
2 white onions (diced)
1 green pepper (chopped)
1 green chilli paste
1 diced tomato
1 tsp ground cumin
1 tsp ground turmeric
1 tsp paprika
1 tsp chilli Powder
2 beef stock cubes GF ** - Can be adapted to Gluten
Free by swapping the highlighted ingredients to GF.
Pinch of salt
2 tbsp rapeseed oil

Base gravy:
1 large tomato (diced)
2 white onions (diced)
⅓ red pepper (diced)
½ tsp each of tomato paste, ground coriander, ground cumin, paprika, turmeric + garam masala
1 tsp each of salt, sugar + garlic and ginger paste
400ml water
GF – Please check spices for 'may contain' ingredient advisories.

Difficulty: Easy/Medium
Ninja® Functions: PRESSURE COOK, SAUTE, SLOW COOK
Freezable: Yes

DIRECTIONS

1. For the base gravy, add the onion, tomato and pepper into the main pot and add the water.
2. PRESSURE COOK for 2 minutes on HI followed by QUICK RELEASE. Add all the other base gravy ingredients. Once everything is brought up to heat, blend down completely into a liquid. Set aside two ladles of the gravy for later.
3. Add the onion, pepper, beef, and green chilli paste to the main pot, then SAUTE in the oil on HI.
4. Add the tomato, cumin, turmeric, paprika and chilli powder, followed by the base gravy and beef stock cubes, and a pinch of salt to taste.
5. PRESSURE COOK for 15 minutes on HI followed by QUICK RELEASE
6. Alternatively, use the SC function set to HI for 4 or more hours and serve with rice.

BEEF BOURGUIGNON

Prep Time - 12/15m	Cook Time - 20m or 3 hrs	Serves - 4	Gluten free✔️☐

INGREDIENTS

1kg diced beef
2 streaky bacon rashers chopped into lardons
1 large white onion (diced)
Handful of mushrooms (sliced)
3 carrots chopped long
2 bay leaves
¾ bottle red wine (merlot recommended)
2 tsp lazy garlic
2 tbsp tomato puree
2 sprigs of thyme
1 tbsp browning
5 beef stock cubes GF ** - Can be adapted to Gluten Free by swapping the highlighted ingredients to GF.
3 tbsp plain flour GF ** - Can be adapted to Gluten Free by swapping the highlighted ingredients to GF.
Pinch of salt
Pinch of black pepper
1 tbsp oil

Difficulty: Easy/Medium
Ninja® Functions: SAUTE, PRESSURE COOK, SLOW COOK
Freezable: Yes

DIRECTIONS

1. Add the beef to the main pot with the onion and the oil. SAUTE on MEDIUM or HI until the beef and onions are browned off and then add in the flour. Stir it all in, then pour in the wine and stir again.
2. Add all the remaining ingredients and stir once more.
3. Switch to PRESSURE COOK on HI and cook for 20 minutes followed by QUICK RELEASE.
4. Alternatively, it may be cooked on SLOW COOK set to HI for approximately 3 hours.
5. Serve with mash or roast potatoes (see Sides/Accompaniments).

DAWN'S CHEEKY CHEATS MEXICAN LASAGNE

Prep Time - 10/12m	Cook Time - 35m	Serves - 4	Gluten free✔☐

INGREDIENTS

1½ lb of minced beef
1 red onion
½ yellow pepper
200g soft cheese
1 tsp easy garlic
1 tsp easy red chilli
2 tbsp fajita spice mix GF – Please check spices for 'may contain' ingredient advisories.
1 tin of chopped tomatoes
3 tbsp tomato paste
150g grated mature cheddar cheese
4 tortillas medium size GF ** - Can be adapted to Gluten Free by swapping the highlighted ingredients to GF.
Handful of chopped mushrooms
2 beef stock cubes GF ** - Can be adapted to Gluten Free by swapping the highlighted ingredients to GF.
2 tbsp honey
½ tsp of salt
150ml water

Difficulty: Easy/Medium
Ninja® Functions: SAUTE, PRESSURE COOK, AIR FRY
Freezable: Yes

DIRECTIONS

1. Select SAUTE function and set to HI or MEDIUM and brown off the meat, tipping out any excess fat.
2. Add the onion, pepper, garlic, chilli, fajita spice mix, chopped tomatoes, tomato paste, mushrooms, beef stock, salt, and water to the main pot.
3. Mix together and PRESSURE COOK for 5 minutes on HI followed by QUICK RELEASE. Once complete, add the honey and stir.
4. Remove the mixture and clean the main pot.
5. Spread a quarter of the cream cheese on to each tortilla in a nice thick layer.
6. Then either in the main pot or in an ovenproof dish, layer it with the first tortilla (with cream cheese already on), and top with some of the meat. Continue until the tortillas and meat are all used finishing with a tortilla which is then topped with the grated cheese.
7. With the assembled lasagne in the machine, select the AIR FRY function set to 200 degrees and cook for 10 minutes, or until the cheese is browned and bubbly.

CHICKEN, BACON AND MUSHROOM CARBONARA

Prep Time - 10/12m	Cook Time - 30/35m	Serves - 4

INGREDIENTS

3 chicken breasts, cut into small pieces
6 bacon rashers, diced small
1 garlic clove, crushed
120g mushrooms chopped
500g linguine
4 egg yolks
1 cup double cream
160g parmesan cheese grated
Salt to taste
Cracked black pepper to top

Tips/Variations (optional):
You can alternatively use a carton of garlic and herb cream cheese with a dash of milk, instead of the yolks and cream, for a different alternative.

Difficulty: Easy/Medium
Ninja® Functions: SAUTE, PRESSURE COOK
Freezable: No

DIRECTIONS

1. Fill the main pot with water up to the 2 cups marker, place the linguine into the pot (I snap in half). PRESSURE COOK on high for 5 minutes, then QR. Lift out and cover to keep warm. Keep a ladle of the leftover water, put aside to cool.
2. SAUTE the chicken, bacon, mushroom and garlic on medium heat until totally cooked through.
3. In a bowl, add a little of the cooled pasta water to the egg yolks, tablespoons at a time, whilst mixing in well. Set aside
4. Once the meats etc. are all cooked, add the linguine, grated parmesan and the cream and bring back to heat for a minute or so on low/medium heat before turning off, add the yolk and pasta water to it whilst stirring, and salt to taste. Serve topped with the remaining cheese and a little cracked black pepper.

HEALTHY SHEPHERD'S PIE

Prep Time - 10m	Cook Time - 30/40m	Serves - 4	Gluten free✔

INGREDIENTS

500g turkey mince
1 diced onion
2 tbsp plain flour GF ** - Can be adapted to Gluten Free by swapping the highlighted ingredients to GF.
¼ bag of spinach
2 beef stock cubes GF ** - Can be adapted to Gluten Free by swapping the highlighted ingredients to GF.
2 chicken stock cubes GF ** - Can be adapted to Gluten Free by swapping the highlighted ingredients to GF.
½ tsp salt
400ml boiling water
3 medium potatoes
1 small celeriac
1 tbsp butter
A dash of milk
1 tbsp oil

Difficulty: Easy/Medium
Ninja® Functions: SAUTE, AIR FRY
Freezable: Yes

DIRECTIONS

1. Place the turkey mince and onion and oil into the main pot using the SAUTE function set to MEDIUM, stirring until cooked through.
2. Add the flour, stir, then add the stock cubes, salt and water, continue to stir it all in until it thickens. Set aside and clean the pot.
3. PRESSURE COOK the chopped potatoes and celeriac for 5 minutes, quick release, then empty the water out, mash with the butter and a dash of milk. Add a pinch of salt to taste.
4. Replace the meat dish and top with the mash, use a fork to spread out and AIR FRY at 200 degrees for 10 minutes to brown off.

CHICKEN, PIZZA STYLE

Prep Time - 15m	Cook Time - 30m	Serves - 4

INGREDIENTS
4 chicken breasts
4 tbsp oil
Handful parmesan
Handful of cheddar
For the tomato topping:
½ carton passata
1 tbsp oil
½ tsp salt
1 tsp garlic
1 tbsp sugar
1 tsp oregano
1 tsp basil
For the breadcrumb coating:
30g parmesan cheese grated
1 cup panko breadcrumbs
1 slice of bread – crumbed
1 tsp garlic powder

Difficulty: Easy/Medium
Ninja® Functions: SAUTE, AIR FRY
Freezable: No

DIRECTIONS

1. In a bowl mix together the ingredients for the tomato topping. Set aside.
2. Now, crumb the sliced bread, add to the panko breadcrumbs, grated cheese and garlic. Set aside.
3. Add 4 tablespoons of oil to the main pot, SAUTE the chicken in the pot until it's browned on each side, then switch to AF function set to 200 degrees and cook for 20 minutes, turning halfway.
4. Top the chicken with the tomato sauce and the cheeses, then the breadcrumbs.
5. AF for a further 5 minutes to melt the cheese and crisp the crumb. Serve

BEEF, BACON AND ONION PIE

Prep Time - 10m	Cook Time - 50m	Serves - 4

INGREDIENTS
1200g diced beef
2 white onions (diced)
½ punnet mushrooms (sliced)
2 rashers of unsmoked bacon (diced)
1 tbsp parsley dried
1 tbsp Bovril®
3 tbsp plain flour
5 beef stock cubes
Salt and pepper to season
1 cup of water
500ml water
1 pack of shortcrust pastry

Difficulty: Easy/Medium
Ninja® Functions: SAUTE, PRESSURE COOK, SLOW COOK, BAKE
Freezable: Yes

DIRECTIONS

1. Add the beef, onion, bacon and mushrooms to the pot, SAUTE until browned off, then fill to 2 cups level with water.
2. PRESSURE COOK on HI for 10 minutes, NATURAL RELEASE for another 10 minutes.
3. Add the stock cubes to a jug with the flour, stir together then add 500ml of boiling water slowly, whilst stirring. It should be stirred into a paste first then gradually loosen it off as you go.
4. Add the gravy mix to the meat, then add salt and pepper to taste, add the parsley and Bovril®. Stir it all in to combine.
5. Grease the tin and place the short-crust pastry inside the base and sides, using a knife to get off the overhang. Using a slotted spoon, add the filling, then add a ladle of gravy over it - the gravy should be nice and thick. Don't add too much, the rest will be used as gravy to go on top. Add the puff pastry to the top of the pie, cutting off any overhang, then brush with milk.
6. Put the tin on the low rack, Cook on bake/roast at 180°C, for 40 minutes. Keep an eye on it. Serve with our chilli chips (see Sides/Accompaniments).

LAMB IN A MINTED LAMB AND CRANBERRY SAUCE

| Prep Time - 8m | Cook Time - 30m | Serves - 4 | Gluten free✔ |

INGREDIENTS
4 lamb steaks
For the gravy:
1 tbsp tomato paste
1 small onion (diced)
1 tbsp plain flour GF ** - Can be adapted to Gluten Free by swapping the highlighted ingredients to GF.
2 tbsp mint sauce
1 tbsp cranberry sauce
3 lamb stock cubes dissolved in 500ml boiling water GF ** - Can be adapted to Gluten Free by swapping the highlighted ingredients to GF.
1 tsp rosemary dried

Difficulty: Easy/Medium
Ninja® Functions: AIR FRY, SAUTE,
Freezable: No

DIRECTIONS

1. Place the lamb steaks on a rack or in the air frying basket and AIR FRY at 200 degrees for 15 to 20 minutes, depending on how you like them.
2. Remove and set aside (cover with foil to keep warm).
3. Select the SAUTE function set to MEDIUM heat. Add the diced onion to the main pot and brown-off, then add flour and stir.
4. Add the lamb stock slowly whilst stirring, then gradually add all other ingredients, continuing to stir. Once everything is mixed together, and the gravy is hot and thick, pour it over the lamb steaks.
5. Serve with mashed or roast potatoes (see Sides/Accompaniments).

GLUTEN FREE TOAD IN THE HOLE WITH MASHED POTATO

Prep Time - 10m	Cook Time - 45/50m	Serves - 4	Gluten Free✔

INGREDIENTS
8 gluten-free sausages
100g corn flour
3 large eggs
150ml whole milk
2 tbsp oil
For the mashed potatoes:
4 large potatoes (peeled and chopped)
Splash of milk
3 tbsp butter
Salt to taste

Difficulty: Easy/Medium
Ninja® Functions: GRILL, AIR FRY, PRESSURE COOK
Freezable: Yes

DIRECTIONS
1. For the batter, measure the milk into a jug, add the eggs and cornflour, then whisk together. Set aside.
2. Select the GRILL function set to MEDIUM and grill the sausages for 5 minutes until browned slightly, but not too much.
3. Remove the sausages and add 2 tablespoons of oil and heat up using the GRILL function set to MEDIUM and heat for 10 minutes.
4. Switch to AIR FRY function set at 180 degrees then quickly add the sausages and pour over batter, done for 22 minutes.
5. Mash, 4 large potatoes chopped up, boiling water up to the number 2 mark in the pot, PRESSURE COOK for 6 minutes on high, quick release. Then mash with a splash of milk, salt and the butter.

JUICY MEATLOAF

Prep Time - 10/15m	Cook Time - 50m	Serves - 4

INGREDIENTS
For the loaf:
2lb ground beef
1 cup salted crackers (or similar)
½ onion
Pinch of salt and pepper
2 tbsp garlic powder
2 tbsp Worcestershire sauce
1 egg
250ml cold water
For the coating:
5 tbsp tomato sauce
5 tsp brown sugar for coating

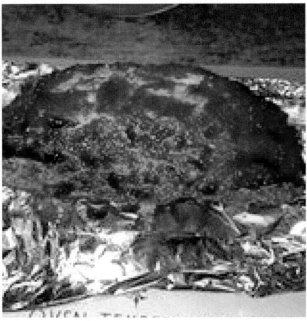

Difficulty: Easy/Medium
Ninja® Functions: AIR FRY, PRESSURE COOK
Freezable: Yes

DIRECTIONS

1. For the loaf, mix all the ingredients together. Mould into a sausage shape and then tightly wrap with cooking foil.
2. Pour the water into the main pot and place the loaf into the air frying basket into the machine. Select the PRESSURE COOK function set to HI and cook for 25 minutes followed by NATURAL RELEASE for 10 minutes, followed by QUICK RELEASE until pressure is fully released.
3. Once PRESSURE COOK is complete, remove the cooking foil from the loaf and smother with half of the sauce and sprinkle on some of the brown sugar.
4. Switch to the AIR FRY function set at 200 degrees for 10 minutes and cook the loaf turning it halfway to coat the other side with the remaining sauce and sugar.

INDIVIDUAL CHICKEN & MUSHROOM PUFF PIE

Prep Time - 15/20m	Cook Time - 45m	Serves - 2

INGREDIENTS
1 tablespoon vegetable oil
4 skinless boneless chicken thighs (chopped into 3 cm squares, seasoned with salt and pepper)
1 onion, halved and sliced
200g baby button mushrooms
A handful of thyme sprigs
200ml chicken stock
100ml milk
500g pack fresh puff pastry, or frozen (defrosted)
1 teaspoon cornflour (mixed with cold water)
1 beaten egg or 2 tablespoons milk for glazing

Difficulty: Medium
Ninja® Functions: SAUTE, PRESSURE COOK, BAKE, AIR FRY
Freezable: Yes

DIRECTIONS

1. For the filling, select the SAUTE function, set to HI and heat the oil. Reduce heat to MEDIUM and add the chicken thighs and SAUTE until sealed.

2. Add in the onion, mushrooms and thyme sprigs and SAUTE on MEDIUM setting for 2 minutes. Ensure that anything that may be stuck to the bottom of the pot has been scraped off and the pot deglazed to avoid receiving the 'ADD WATER' notification. Add in the milk and chicken stock, place the PRESSURE COOK lid onto the machine and set the valve to SEAL and select PRESSURE COOK function on LOW for 5 minutes followed by NATUAL RELEASE for 5 minutes.

3. Switch to SAUTE function and add in the cornflour and continue to SAUTE on medium setting until the filling has thickened. Spoon the filling into an ovenproof pie dish with a lip that fits the machine being used and leave to cool.

4. For the pie, roll out the pastry to a thickness of two £1 coins on a floured surface. Using either beaten egg, or milk, brush the lip of the dish and then lift the pastry over the filling and gently press onto the dish with your fingers. Trim any excess pastry with a knife. Brush the pie with either egg, or milk to glaze.

5. Select the BAKE function and set at 180 degrees. Place the pie dish on a rack or silicone mat and bake for 10 minutes. Switch to AIR FRY function set at 180 degrees and cook for a further 5 minutes until the pastry is golden brown.
   Serve with creamy mashed potato or roast potatoes (see Sides/Accompaniments).

ASHA'S 'FABULICIOUS' LANCASHIRE HOTPOT

Prep Time - 15/20m	Cook Time - 60m	Serves - 2/3

INGREDIENTS

1 tbsp vegetable oil
500g lamb (not too lean and diced)
2 brown onions (peeled and sliced thinly)
300ml hot lamb stock
2 bay leaves
½ tsp salt
½ tsp ground black pepper
1 tsp garlic granules
1 tsp dried mint
A few dashes of Worcestershire sauce
2 large-sized carrots (peeled, cut into thick half-moons)
1 tsp cornflour (mixed with water to avoid lumps)
4 medium-sized potatoes (peeled, sliced into 2-3mm slices)
1 tsp dried rosemary
Vegetable oil to coat potato slices

Difficulty: Medium
Ninja® Functions: SAUTE, PRESSURE COOK, ROAST, AIR FRY
Freezable: Yes

DIRECTIONS

1. Select the SAUTE function set to HI and heat the oil. Reduce to MEDIUM setting and add in the lamb and onions and SAUTE for 3-4 minutes until the lamb has browned.

2. Add in the stock, bay leaves, salt, pepper, garlic granules, and dried mint. Give everything a stir and ensure anything that may be stuck to the bottom of the pot has been scraped off to deglaze the main pot and avoid receiving the 'ADD WATER' notification. Place the PRESSURE COOK lid onto the machine and set the valve to SEAL and select PRESSURE COOK function and set to HI for 10 minutes, followed by QUICK RELEASE by moving the valve to VENT position immediately after the timer has finished counting down.

3. Tip in the carrots and add in a few dashes of Worcestershire sauce. Set PRESSURE COOK to LOW and cook for 5 minutes followed by NATURAL RELEASE for 5 minutes. Once complete, switch to SAUTE function on medium and stir in the cornflour and frozen peas for a few minutes to thicken the mixture.

4. Transfer the mixture to an ovenproof dish that fits the machine. Layer on the sliced potatoes. Brush/spray the potatoes with vegetable oil and sprinkle on the dried rosemary. Place the dish into the machine and select ROAST function set at 160 degrees and cook for 20 minutes.

5. Switch to AIR FRY function at 180 degrees and cook for a further for 5 minutes – add additional time to brown/crisp the potatoes to preferred liking.

PEPPERED STEAK BAKE & PAPRIKA WEDGES & GRAVY

Prep Time - 20m	Cook Time - 40/50m	Serves - 6

INGREDIENTS

2 packs of ready-rolled puff pastry
1.5lb steak meat (chopped small)
2 onions (diced)
3 tbsp plain flour
4 beef stock cubes
½ tbsp Bovril®
1 tsp salt
½ tsp ground black pepper
700 ml water (boiled)
1 tbsp milk
1 tbsp oil
For the wedges:
6 medium-sized potatoes (wedged)
1 tbsp each of oil and paprika
Pinch of salt

Difficulty: Medium
Ninja® Functions: SAUTE, PRESSURE COOK, AIR FRY
Freezable: Yes

DIRECTIONS

1. On SAUTE, MEDIUM heat brown-off the beef and onions in the oil. Add in the flour and stir. Then add the boiling water to the crumbled stock cubes, stir and pour over the meat, stirring as you add. Add the Bovril®, salt and pepper. PRESSURE COOK for 15 minutes on LOW, then NATURAL RELEASE until pressure is fully released. Using a straining spoon, remove the meat from the gravy, place into a separate bowl and the gravy in a jug. (Add a little cornflour mixed with water to the gravy if it needs thickening).

2. Clean out the main pot. Remove the pastry from its packaging, but leave it on the parchment it's wrapped in, and cut each pack into 6, so you have 12 equal squares. Spoon the beef onto 6 of the pastry squares adding the other 6 pastry squares to the top. Using a fork, seal the edges of the pastry squares together. Cut the parchment around the steak bake, and brush each with milk. Place the bakes on the parchment into the machine. Stacking as many as you can. AIR FRY at 180 degrees for 10 minutes. Meanwhile, wash and pat dry the potato wedges and then coat in oil, season them with salt and the paprika. When the steak bakes are ready, take out and set aside. Place the wedges into the air frying basket and AIR FRY at 200 degrees for 20 minutes, stirring a couple of times. You can place the steak bake on top of the chips for the last 3 minutes to bring back to heat. Heat the gravy in the main pot whilst serving the steak and chips, pour over your meal.

STEAK DIANE

Prep Time - 8/10m	Cook Time - 18/25m	Serves - 2/4

INGREDIENTS

2-4 steaks of your choice (oiled)
1 large white onion (sliced or diced)
130g mushrooms (chestnut are best)
1 tbsp olive oil
1 garlic clove
1 tbsp Worcestershire sauce
2 tsp dijon mustard
½ cup of brandy
200ml double cream
200ml creme fraiche
Pinch salt and pepper

Difficulty: Medium
Ninja® Functions: GRILL, SAUTE
Freezable: No

DIRECTIONS

1. For the steaks: season the steaks with oil, salt and pepper. Select the GRILL function set to 240 and heat for a few minutes, then add the steaks to the high shelf, cook for 4 minutes each side. (this recipe used a thin rib eye steak, cooked to medium). Take out and set aside to rest for 5 minutes.

2. For the sauce: on SAUTE, MEDIUM heat, cook mushrooms, onion and garlic in the olive oil until browned off. Turn down to low/medium and add the brandy and flambé if you're brave enough! It should take around 20-30 seconds, then when the flame is almost gone, stir. Add the dijon, Worcester sauce and finally the cream and creme fraiche, then add salt to taste.

3. Serve the steak and pour over the Diane sauce.

4. Serve with little square roasted potatoes with herbs like rosemary, parsley or thyme.

SONIA'S TANTALISING PORK EGG FRIED RICE

Prep Time - 8/10m	Cook Time - 20m	Serves - 2

Ingredients
1 tbsp of unsalted butter
200g of pork luncheon meat (cubed)
3 cloves garlic (chopped)
1 cup frozen vegetables
1 cup of pre-cooked basmati rice
1 tbsp light soy sauce
2 beaten eggs
1 tbsp oil

Difficulty: Easy
Ninja® Functions: SAUTE
Freezable: No

DIRECTIONS

1. Add the butter into the pan and SAUTE on low to medium heat, allow to melt down. Add the pork luncheon meat in and cook for a few minutes until heated through and slightly brown.
2. Put the garlic and frozen veg into the pot, stir until they are well combined and the veg is heated through.
3. Add the rice and toss and fry until well incorporated and rice heated through. Pour the soy sauce in and stir. Push rice to one side of the pan.
4. Add oil and beaten egg, cook till scrambled and lastly mix all together.

RISOTTO BOLOGNESE

Prep Time - 8/10m	Cook Time - 25/3m	Serves - 2

INGREDIENTS

1 packet mince meat (around 500g)
1 small onion (chopped)
1 tbsp mixed herbs
1 tbsp oregano
1 tsp soy sauce
1 tsp Worcestershire sauce
2 beef stock cubes
1 beef stock pot
4 tbsp tomato puree
4 tbsp garlic puree
Pinch of salt and pepper
375ml carton tomato passata
450ml water
1 cups of rice

Difficulty: Easy
Ninja® Functions: SAUTE, PRESSURE COOK
Freezable: No

DIRECTIONS

1. Set machine to SAUTE on medium to low heat, and SAUTE the mince and onion to brown. Add mixed herbs, oregano, soy and Worcestershire sauce, and stir.
2. Add beef stock cubes, beef stock pot, and salt and pepper to taste. Now turn off.
3. Add 4 tablespoons each of tomato purée and garlic purée, add passata and stir. Pour in the water, then sprinkle the rice over the top and PRESSURE COOK for 3 minutes, then NATURAL RELEASE for 5 minutes.
4. Give it a good stir and enjoy!

SLOW COOK BEEF (DONENESS - WELL)

Prep Time - less than 15 m	Cook Time - 4 hrs	Serves - 2/3	Gluten Free✔☐

INGREDIENTS

680g beef joint (topside)
Olive oil (spray)
1 tbsp all-purpose seasoning GF – Please check spices for 'may contain' ingredient advisories.
1 tsp dried rosemary
Beef stock (500ml made with boiled water) GF ** - Can be adapted to Gluten Free by swapping the highlighted ingredients to GF.
4 shallots (peeled and halved)
2 garlic cloves (peeled and halved)

Tips/Variations (optional):
If your machine does not have the SEAR function, step 1 may be done in a pan on the hob. Use the PRESSURE COOK lid set to vent or a glass lid that fits.

Difficulty: Easy/Medium
Ninja® Functions: SAUTE, SLOW COOK
Freezable: Yes (sliced recommended)

DIRECTIONS

1. Create a rub by mixing together the all-purpose seasoning and the dried rosemary.
2. Spray the beef joint with olive oil and massage into the meat by hand.
3. Sprinkle the rub over the meat and spread all over by hand to coat the joint.
4. Select the SAUTE function and set to HI to heat up the main pot.
5. Once heated, place the beef joint into the pot and move around to seal and sear all sides and brown off.
6. Pour the beef stock into the pot and drop in the shallots and garlic. Bring the contents of the pot up to boil. Switch the machine to SC function and set to high.
7. Cover the pot with the PRESSURE COOK lid with the valve set to VENT, or a glass lid, and leave the joint to slow cook for 3½ hours. The glass lid allows you to peer in and see what is going on in there without having to take it off during cooking.
8. Once the cooking time is complete, remove the joint from the machine and cover with foil and leave to rest for 10 minutes before carving and serving.

BEEF BRISKET (DONENESS: WELL)

Prep Time - 15/20m	Cook Time - 3hrs	Serves - ¾ for this weight	Gluten Free✔

INGREDIENTS
800-900g brisket joint
Olive oil (spray)
1 tbsp all-purpose Seasoning GF – Please check spices for 'may contain' ingredient advisories.
1 tsp garlic granules
1 tsp onion granules
2 tsp cold water

Tips/Variations (optional):
If your machine does not have the SEAR function, step 1 may be done in a pan on the hob

Difficulty: Medium
Ninja® Functions: SAUTE, ROAST
Freezable: Yes (sliced recommended)

DIRECTIONS

1. Create a rub by mixing together the all-purpose seasoning, garlic granules, and onion granules.
2. Spray the beef joint with olive oil and massage into the meat by hand.
3. Sprinkle the rub over the meat and spread all over by hand to coat the joint and leave for an hour at room temperature. Select the SAUTE function and set to HI to heat up the main pot.
4. Once heated, place the beef joint in the pot and move around to seal and sear all sides. Wash the main pot before using for the next step if continuing to cook in the same machine.
5. Using thick and strong cooking foil, create a foil parcel and place the beef joint into it with the cold water. Ensure the foil is secured and tucked in to prevent it from flying up and blocking the fan.
6. Select the ROAST function on the machine and set to 200 degrees and leave to preheat for 3 minutes, or until the 'ADD FOOD' notification appears.
7. Reduce the temperature to 130 degrees and place the beef joint on a silicone mat into the machine – you can place it in a tin on the low rack if you prefer, to catch the juices for a gravy). Leave the joint to cook for 2½ hours. Remove the joint from the machine and leave in foil to rest for 15 minutes before carving and serving.

ROASTED CHICKEN THIGHS

Prep Time - 15m + 1 hr marinating	Cook Time - 20m	Serves - 2	Gluten Free✔️

INGREDIENTS

4 chicken thighs (gashed with skin on and bone in)
1 tbsp all-purpose seasoning GF – Please check spices for 'may contain' ingredient advisories.
1 tsp dried thyme
1 tsp garlic granules
½ a lemon (juice only)

Difficulty: Easy
Ninja® Functions: ROAST, AIR FRY
Freezable: Yes, in slices

DIRECTIONS

1. Create a rub by mixing together the all-purpose seasoning, dried thyme and garlic granules.
2. Roll the gashed chicken one piece at a time in the rub to coat and then rub all over by hand getting under the skin and into the gashes. Place in a bowl and leave at room temperature for 1-2 hours before cooking.
3. Select the ROAST function on the machine, place the air frying basket into it and set to 180 degrees and preheat for 3 minutes or until the 'ADD FOOD' notification appears.
4. Remove the chicken from the cling film and squeeze the juice of the lemon over it.
5. Place the chicken directly into the air frying basket and cook for 15 minutes.
6. Switch to AIR FRY function and set to 200 degrees and then cook the chicken for a further 3 to 5 minutes until the skin is browned and crispy.
7. Note: Cooking time may need to be adjusted depending on size of chicken thighs. Check by piercing the chicken in the thickest part and ensuring the juices run clear.
8. Serve with chips and salad or as part of a roast dinner and enjoy!

AMY'S AMAZING BOTTOMLESS PIZZA

Prep Time – 10m	Cook Time – 20m	Serves - 2/4	Gluten Free✔

INGREDIENTS

Here's what I used, but you can use any selection of veg and meat you like.

Mixed peppers
Red onion
Handful of mushrooms
Chillies
Spring onions
Slice of ham
Handful of cooked chicken
Pepperoni
A jar of tomato and chilli pasta sauce*
Grated mozzarella
Ball of mozzarella.

Tips/Variations (optional):

Use gluten free sauces gluten, most pasta sauces are naturally gluten free but just check the ingredients and may contain warnings, also double check the meat has no warnings too.

Difficulty: Easy
Ninja® Functions: GRILL
Freezable: YES

DIRECTIONS

1. On a MEDIUM GRILL setting, find a dish that will fit inside the Ninja® being used. Put a few of each topping to one side that you would like to scatter on the top later on, then put the rest of the veg in the tin (apart from the spring onions) with a little oil and grill for 3 minutes.

2. Add in the meat and spring onions and GRILL for 3 further minutes. Next add enough of a jar of sauce so that it comes just to the top of the ingredients and cook for a further 6 minutes to heat through.

3. Then add grated mozzarella and slices of a mozzarella ball on top and GRILL for a further 3 minutes until it just starts to brown.

4. Finally top with pepperoni, chillies and the green ends of spring onions and GRILL for a further 4minutes or until browned to preference.

YORKSHIRE PUDDING

Prep Time - 5/8m	Cook Time - 25/35m	Serves - 4/6	Vegetarian (V)

INGREDIENTS
½ cup plain flour
½ cup milk
3 x eggs
3/4 tbsp vegetable oil

Tips/Variations:
Whilst the Yorkshire mix is cooking, it's really important that you don't peak as it sinks the Yorkshire. And the oil needs to be piping hot too, hence the timings.

GRILL IN TIN X 6

FOODI IN LARGE TIN

DUAL

Difficulty: Medium
Ninja® Functions: GRILL, AIR FRY, BAKE/ROAST
Freezable: Yes

DIRECTIONS

1. **FOODI/GRILL:** Heat the oil (3 tbsp) in a deep cake tin on the low rack (if using the Foodi), GRILL on HI for 9 minutes.

2. Place the flour and eggs in a bowl and whisk, gradually add the milk slowly, (alternatively I just throw it all in my blender and whizz it for 10 seconds) whilst the Ninja® heats the oil

3. Put the mix in the fridge. When the oil is heated, pour the mixture into a tin and cook on BAKE at 190 degrees for 25 minutes. This is for making 1 large or 6 small. Don't open the machine to look though, otherwise it ruins the Yorkshires!

4. **DUAL:** Add all the above ingredients apart from the dripping to the blender or whisk together.   Add 2 tbsp of oil to each side of the Dual, and on MAX CRISP at 240 degrees, cook for 8 minutes. Keep the mix cold in the fridge whilst you're doing this. Add the half the batter to each side and cook on bake for 18 minutes on 190 degrees. Once again, no peeking! Serve with a roast or bangers and mash.

STEW AND DUMPLINGS

Prep Time - 15/20m	Cook Time – 30m	Serves - 4/6

INGREDIENTS
750g diced beef
1 onion (diced)
2 carrots (chopped)
2 rashers of streaky bacon (diced)
2 tbsp sage
1 tbsp salt
2 tbsp tomato paste
2 tbsp Worcester sauce
4 beef stock cubes
2 tsp of Bovril®
¼ carton passata
240g suet
480g self-raising flour, extra for covering dumplings
600ml water
2 tbsp plain flour

Difficulty: Medium
Ninja® Functions: SAUTE, PRESSURE COOK
Freezable: Yes

DIRECTIONS

1. Add the beef, onion and bacon to the pot, and brown-off on SAUTE. Add the carrots, sage, tomato paste and 2 tablespoons of plain flour, Bovril®, stir to thicken before adding 4 stock cubes in 600ml of water.

2. Add the passata, Worcester sauce and bay leaves to the pot. PRESSURE COOK on high for 10 minutes followed by QUICK RELEASE.

3. For the dumplings, add the suet and self-raising flour together, add water slowly until it's bound together but a little sticky, then get some of the remaining flour and put it on your hands, take around ⅛ of the mix and, using flour to dust, make a ball and set aside, do this with the rest of the mix.

4. Add to the stew mix and PRESSURE COOK on HI for 10 minutes followed by NATURAL RELEASE until pressure is fully released and serve.

CHILLI CON CARNE

Prep Time - 10/12m	Cook Time – 20m	Serves - 4

INGREDIENTS

500g minced beef
1 can kidney beans (optional)
1 onion (diced)
1 tsp olive oil
1 tin chopped tomatoes, refill halfway with water
2 beef stock cubes
1 garlic clove
2 tbsp Worcester sauce
3 tbsp tomato paste
2 tsp chilli
2 tsp paprika
2 tsp cumin
2 tsp coriander
2 tbsp honey
Salt and black pepper to taste

Difficulty: Medium
Ninja® Functions: SAUTE, PRESSURE COOK
Freezable: Yes

DIRECTIONS

1. On SAUTE, MEDIUM heat, add the chopped onion until browned in the oil, add the minced beef, and brown. Empty out any excess fat.
2. Then add the rest of the ingredients, including the ½ can of water after putting the chopped toms in. Add everything apart from seasoning and PRESSURE COOK on HI for 5 minutes followed by QUICK RELEASE.
3. Add salt and pepper to taste.
4. Serve with rice and top with cheese if desired.

SPAGHETTI BOLOGNESE

Prep Time – 15m	Cook Time – 25m	Serves – 2/4

INGREDIENTS
500g lean minced beef
1 tbsp olive oil
2 unsmoked bacon rashers, cut up small
1 onion (diced)
1 tsp salt
2 garlic cloves (crushed)
2 tsp oregano
1 tsp basil
3 tbsp tomato paste
1 tin chopped tomatoes
500g carton of passata
2 beef stock cubes
1 tbsp honey
4 sun-dried tomatoes in oil, finely chopped
½ sprig of fresh rosemary (chopped)
1 glass red wine (large) or veg stock in
300ml water
Parmesan to top
250g spaghetti

Difficulty: Medium
Ninja® Functions: SAUTE, PRESSURE COOK
Freezable: Yes

DIRECTIONS

1. Select the SAUTE function set to MEDIUM and add the onion, garlic and chopped bacon rashers until slightly golden in colour. Add the minced beef and brown-off. Then add the chopped tomatoes, tomato paste, oregano, basil, beef stock cubes, rosemary, sun-dried tomatoes, salt and honey, passata and red wine. Mix this all together.
2. Place the spaghetti in a cake tin and cover with water. Put the low rack into the main pot with the Bolognese, with the spaghetti in the tin on the shelf.
3. PRESSURE COOK on HI for 5 minutes, followed by QUICK RELEASE.
4. Serve with a sprinkling of parmesan and a little fresh rosemary.

STICKY RIBS

Prep Time – 10m	Cook Time - 50m	Serves - 2/4	Gluten Free✔

INGREDIENTS
Pork ribs 1.4kg
Sticky rib/wing sauce of choice GF – Please check spices for 'may contain' ingredient advisories.

Difficulty: Easy
Ninja® Functions: PRESSURE COOK, AIR FRY
Freezable: No

DIRECTIONS

1. Pour boiling water up to the number 2 inside the main pot and place the air frying basket into the machine and stack the ribs inside.

2. Select the PRESSURE COOK function set to HI for 25 minutes and cook the ribs. Complete the process with NATURAL RELEASE for 15 minutes. (This took about 15 minutes).

3. Carefully remove the ribs from the air frying basket and give the pot and basket a quick wash. Coat the ribs in the sauce (save some to keep brushing on whilst cooking).

4. Place a piece of greaseproof paper or foil in the bottom of the air frying basket to catch the sauce.

5. Put the ribs back in and AIR FRY at 180 degrees for about 12 minutes or until cooked to your liking, tossing them about during this time and recoating with the sauce twice.

Packet Mixes

This section is designed to help take the guesswork out of what functions to use when translating the back of packet instructions (e.g. 'on the hob' or 'place in the oven') at times when we want to smash out a quick meal for convenience to save time, but still want to attempt it in our Dream Machine.

COTTAGE PIE PACKET MIX

Prep Time - 20/30m	Cook Time - 35m	Serves - As per packet

INGREDIENTS
As per back-of-packet instructions
Mashed Potato – see
Sides/Accompaniments

Tips/Variations (optional):
Add 1 teaspoon of garlic granules, 2 squirts
of brown sauce, a handful or two of grated
cheese. A good batch cook recipe.

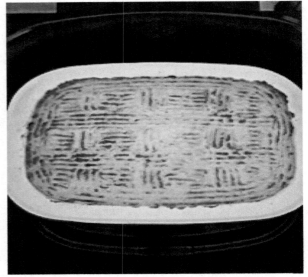

Difficulty: Medium
Ninja® Functions: SAUTE, BAKE, AIR FRY
Freezable: Yes

DIRECTIONS

1. Prepare the filling using the SAUTE function switching between HI, MEDIUM/HI and LOW settings – just as if it were being prepared in a pan on the hob and adjusting the heat.
2. Add in the garlic granules and brown sauce (if using).
3. Transfer filling to ovenproof dish and top with mashed potato and cook using BAKE function set at 180 degrees for 20 minutes. Score the mash potato with a fork for a crispy finish.
4. Sprinkle grated cheese (if using) over the pie and switch the machine to AIR FRY function set at 180 degrees and cook for a further 5 minutes – or until the cheese is brown and bubbly to your liking.
5. Serve with steamed green veg and enjoy!

CHICKEN CHASSEUR PACKET MIX

Prep Time - 10/15m	Cook Time - 50m	Serves - As per packet

INGREDIENTS
As per back-of-packet instructions
Tips/Variations:
Chicken thighs cut into 4cm pieces, add in
1/2 teaspoon chilli flakes (optional). Oven
step on back of packet instructions
omitted.

Difficulty: Easy
Ninja® Functions: SAUTE
Freezable: Yes

DIRECTIONS

1. Cook the chicken (cut into pieces), mushrooms, and onions together in a little oil using the SAUTE function and switching between HI and MEDIUM settings as required - just as if it were being prepared in a pan on the hob and adjusting the heat until the chicken is sealed and the onions are soft.
2. Add in the tomato puree to the seasoning mix (stir in chilli flakes if using).
3. Continue on SAUTE function on low setting for 40 minutes with occasional stirring.
4. Serve with thyme roasted chantenay carrots and baby new potatoes and enjoy!

CHILLI CON CARNE PACKET MIX

Prep Time - 20/30m	Cook Time - 40m	Serves - As per packet

INGREDIENTS
As per back-of-packet instructions
Tips/Variations:
This is a good batch-cook recipe!

Difficulty: Easy
Ninja® Functions: SAUTE
Freezable: Yes

DIRECTIONS

1. Using the SAUTE function and switching between HI, MEDIUM/HI and LOW settings – just as if it were being prepared in a pan on the hob and adjusting the heat, SAUTE the ingredients as per packet until cooked through.
2. Using the SAUTE function with the heat set to MEDIUM/LOW and leave to simmer away until fully cooked and flavours developed.
3. Serve with rice or potato wedges see Sides/Accompaniments and enjoy!

DONER KEBAB PACKET MIX

Prep Time - 8/10m	Cook Time - 40m	Serves - As per pecket

INGREDIENTS
As per back-of-packet instructions

Tips/Variations:
Blitz the meat mixture through a blender until it has a paste-like consistency. 20% fat minced lamb gives a more authentic taste and texture experience.

Difficulty: Easy
Ninja® Functions: BAKE, AIR FRY
Freezable: Yes (sliced recommended)

DIRECTIONS

1. Whilst preparing the meat, it is recommended to blitz the ingredients together in a blender until the mixture resembles a paste-like consistency.
2. Form the meat into a giant sausage shape, cover in cling film and place in the fridge for a few hours. This will allow the flavours of the seasoning to really infuse the meat for a full-on flavour experience.
3. To cook the meat, remove the cling film and tightly wrap it in thick cooking foil, select the BAKE function and set at 180 degrees. Place the meat in an ovenproof dish either on a low rack, or silicone mat in your machine and cook for 25 minutes.
4. Remove the foil (remember to be careful as it will be very hot) and select the AIR FRY function set at 180 degrees and cook the meat for a further 5 minutes.
5. Remove from the machine and leave to rest for 10 minutes before slicing and serving.
6. A fabulous fakeaway!

Sauces/Rubs/Marinades

BLENDED HEALTHY PASTA SAUCE

Prep Time - 6m	Cook Time - 10m	Serves - 3/4	Gluten Free✔

Ingredients

1 tin of tomatoes

1 tsp chopped garlic

1 tbsp tomato puree

1 beef stock GF ** - Can be adapted to Gluten Free by swapping the highlighted ingredients to GF.

1 chicken stock GF ** - Can be adapted to Gluten Free by swapping the highlighted ingredients to GF.

½ tsp salt

1 tsp oregano

1 tbsp tomato ketchup

1 onion

Handful of mixed peppers

¼ chopped leek

2 tbsp peas

Difficulty: Easy

Ninja® Functions: BLENDER, SOUPMAKER, PRESSURE COOK

Freezable: Yes

DIRECTIONS

1. Add all the above ingredients to a blender, and blend on auto IQ or until smooth. Pour over the cooked pasta. Then SAUTE and bring to heat.
2. White pasta - cover in water, PRESSURE COOK on HI for 4 minutes followed by QUICK RELEASE.
3. Brown pasta – cover in water, PRESSURE COOK on HI for 9 minutes followed by QUICK RELEASE.
4. This can also be used as Bolognese sauce, pasta sauce, pizza-base sauce, chilli sauce (just add 1 teaspoon of chilli paste/powder) or in portobello stuffed mushrooms.
5. Add to chicken with cheese on top.

CHEESE SAUCE

Prep Time - 6/8m	Cook Time - 8/10m	Serves - 3/4

INGREDIENTS
30g plain flour
40g butter
Pinch of salt to taste
½ pint of milk
50g parmesan cheese
75g cheddar cheese

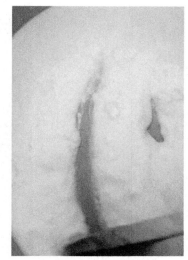

Difficulty: Easy/Medium
Ninja® Functions: SAUTE
Freezable: No

DIRECTIONS

1. Select the SAUTE function set to LOW/MEDIUM heat and melt the butter.
2. Add in the flour and a pinch of salt and stir into a paste.
3. Gradually add the milk, a dash at a time and stir until that dash is mixed in. Keep adding a little more and stir until it's all been added, then add the cheese.
4. Increase the SAUTE setting to MEDIUM whilst continuing to stir, then turn off the heat.
5. This sauce may be used on cauliflower cheese, macaroni, or as the white sauce in a lasagne.

BBQ GRAVY

Prep Time - 8/10m	Cook Time - 10m	Serves - 2/3

INGREDIENTS
1 onion (sliced)
1 tbsp oil
1 tbsp plain flour
1 tbsp Worcester sauce
1 tbsp brown sugar
3 tbsp BBQ sauce
2 tbsp tomato paste
1 tsp Bovril®
250ml boiling water

Difficulty: Easy
Ninja® Functions: SAUTE
Freezable: No

DIRECTIONS

1. Place the sliced onion into the main pot with the oil and SAUTE on MEDIUM heat. When browned-off, turn off the heat and add in the flour and stir. Then add in the Bovril® and sugar.
2. Slowly pour in the boiling water whilst stirring, starting with a small amount first to make it into a paste, then gradually add more water to loosen the mixture until it is all used up.
3. Select the SAUTE function again and set to MEDIUM heat. Add the remaining ingredients whilst stirring.
4. Can be served with cooked chicken thighs, but it also complements sausage and mash, or on roast potatoes.

BBQ SAUCE/MARINADE & RUB FOR RIBS, CHICKEN, PORK

Prep Time - 15/20m	Cook Time - 0m	Serves - 2/4

INGREDIENTS
For the rub:
2 tsp brown sugar
1 tsp chilli powder
1 tsp cumin
1 tsp garlic powder
1 tsp onion powder
1 tsp smoked paprika
Pinch of ground black pepper.
For the marinade:
3 tbsp BBQ sauce
2 tbsp honey
½ tbsp malt vinegar
1 tsp garlic powder
1 tsp tomato paste
1 tsp paprika
½ tsp onion powder
½ tsp salt
Pinch of black pepper

Difficulty: Easy/Medium
Ninja® Functions: NONE
Freezable: Yes (for the marinade, defrost overnight before use)

DIRECTIONS

1. Mix together the ingredients for the rub, then add a little oil to the meat and sprinkle on top. The rub can either be used as a dry mix or, it may be added to some of the BBQ sauce/marinade onto the meat before AIR FRYING.

2. Alternatively, you could use just the BBQ sauce/marinade to marinate the meat from the night before cooking and cook with the marinade only on the meat.

3. Both of the above can be stored for further use; the rub is fine in a jar for a couple of months, and the marinade will last in the fridge for up to five days.

FAJITA SEASONING MIX

Prep Time - 6/8m	Cook Time - 0m	Serves - 4/8	Vegetarian ✓	Gluten Free ✓

INGREDIENTS

2 tbsp paprika

½ tsp onion powder

1 tbsp garlic powder

1 tbsp cumin

½ tbsp chilli powder mild

½ tbsp coriander powder

1 tbsp oregano

1 tsp sugar

1 tsp salt

GF – Please check spices for 'may contain' ingredient advisories.

Difficulty: Easy

Ninja® Functions: NONE

Freezable: No

DIRECTIONS

1. Mix together all the ingredients and store in a jar.
2. This may be used in Mexican dishes, omelettes, over chips, on chicken thighs, with some honey, and on chicken breasts with some cheese.

SWEET CHILLI JAM (HOT)

Prep Time - 10m	Cook Time - 40m	Vegetarian ✓

INGREDIENTS
3 small shallots
120g red chilli
4 tsp garlic paste
400g white sugar
50ml water
1 lime-worth of juice
80ml malt vinegar

Difficulty: Easy
Ninja® Functions: SAUTE, PRESSURE COOK
Freezable: No

DIRECTIONS

1. Chop the shallots and chilli up very finely.
2. Then throw all the above ingredients into the main pot, and SAUTE on MEDIUM heat, just enough to liquify the sugar.
3. Switch SAUTE, LOW/MEDIUM to slightly thicken the mixture, around 10 minutes. As it cools it will thicken even more.
4. Cool and store in a glass jar.

Desserts/Puddings/Cakes

GLUTEN FREE LEMON MERINGUE PIE

| Prep Time - 50m | Cook Time - 25m | Serves - 6/8 | Vegetarian ✔ | Gluten Free ✔ |

INGREDIENTS - (I used a 23cm flan dish)
For the pastry:
300g gluten-free plain flour
3 tbsp caster sugar
145g unsalted butter (cubed)
1½ tsp xanthan gum
2 large eggs
For the filling:
3 large eggs (just yolks)
175ml water
2 tbsp cornflour
50g caster sugar
25g butter
2 lemons (zest and juice)
For the meringue:
3 egg whites (from the filling) + 150g caster sugar

Difficulty: Medium
Ninja® Functions: BAKE, SAUTE
Freezable: No

DIRECTIONS

1. For the pastry case, put all the pastry ingredients in a bowl apart from the eggs. Rub all the butter in until it resembles breadcrumbs.
2. Beat the eggs and gradually add in, mix together until it forms a dough. Wrap in cling film and chill for at least half an hour.
3. Roll out on a floured surface until about ½cm thick, then pick it up over your rolling pin and put on top of tin. Press it into the edges of the tin carefully, and make sure to leave an overhang as it shrinks slightly.
4. Prick the base with a fork, put baking paper inside, add baking beans, and BAKE for 15 minutes at 150 degrees. Remove the baking beans, egg wash the pastry and put it back in for 10 minutes. Take it out, trim the edges and leave to cool slightly.
5. For the filling, Grate the lemon zest. Then, in the main pot add the lemon zest and juice of both lemons, plus all other ingredients apart from the butter. Mix it together until it is smooth and there are no lumps. SAUTE, on MEDIUM heat, add butter and keep mixing until it boils and thickens up. Pour into the pastry case and leave it to cool and set.
6. In a bowl, Whisk the egg whites until they form stiff peaks, then gradually add the sugar in, whisk until the meringue is glossy, and you can hold it upside-down over your head. Add it on top of the lemon filling and BAKE at 120 degrees for about 50 minutes until nicely browned and crispy. Leave to completely cool before slicing.

GLUTEN FREE CRUNCHIE® CAKES

Prep Time - 15/20m	Cook Time - 13/15m	Serves - 12	Vegetarian ✓	Gluten Free ✓

Ingredients

For cake:
175g gluten-free self-raising flour
175g caster sugar
175g softened butter/margarine
3 large eggs
¼ tsp xanthan gum
½ tsp baking powder
½ tsp vanilla extract

For the filling and topping:
Crunchie® spread
2 *Crunchies®*

For the buttercream icing:
250g unsalted butter
500g icing sugar
Splash of milk

Difficulty: Medium
Ninja® Functions: BAKE
Freezable: No

DIRECTIONS

1. Cream together the sugar and butter, then beat the eggs and add in along with the flour, vanilla extract, baking powder, and xanthan gum. Give it all a good mix until well combined. Spoon the mixture into cupcake cases.

2. BAKE at 160°C for 13-15 minutes. Insert a skewer into the centre of the cake, and if it comes out clean the cake is properly cooked.

3. Leave to cool on a wire rack then, using a pastry cutter, cut a small circle out the middle of each cake. Trim the underneath of the circle you take out so you are just left with the top, scoop the extra bit of cake out the hole and press down gently.

4. Mix the *Crunchie®* spread with a splash of milk until it's a smoother consistency, like melted chocolate, and then fill each hole with it. Pop the little circle of cake back on top.

5. To make the icing, cut the butter into small cubes and beat it until it is soft and pale in colour. Add in the icing sugar gradually and mix until fully combined, then add the vanilla extract and give another quick mix.

6. If it's still quite thick then add a small splash of milk, mix again and check until you have a good consistency to pipe with.

7. Fill the piping bag and pipe onto each cake, or you could just spread it on instead. Crush the *Crunchie®* bars in a food bag and then sprinkle on top.

CHOCOLATE CAKE

Prep Time - 10m	Cook Time - 55m	Serves - 6/8	Vegetarian ✓

INGREDIENTS

Just under 160g self-raising flour, topped up with 10g cocoa powder

170g margarine

170g caster sugar

3 eggs

For the chocolate icing topping:

Fresh cream to fill, add 1 tbsp cocoa powder and 1 tbsp icing sugar to make chocolate flavoured filling.

Top with melted chocolate

Difficulty: Easy/Medium

Ninja® Functions: BAKE

Freezable: No

DIRECTIONS

1. Cream together the sugar and margarine, whisk, then add the rest of the ingredients and whisk again until the mixture is lighter in colour.
2. Line an 8x3" cake tin with parchment just on the bottom and pour the mixture in.
3. Place the tin on the low rack in the main pot. Select the BAKE function set at 140 degrees for 55 minutes. Leave to cool.
4. In the meantime, select the SAUTE function set to LOW/MEDIUM setting, and slowly melt the chocolate, constantly stirring.
5. Cut the cake in half and fill the inside with whisked fresh cream and top with the melted chocolate.

CORNFLAKE TART

Prep Time - 10m	Cook Time - 35m	Serves - 6/8	Vegetarian

INGREDIENTS
320g shortcrust pastry
50g butter
125g golden syrup
25g dark brown sugar
100g jam
100g cornflakes

Difficulty: Easy/Medium
Ninja® Functions: BAKE, SAUTE
Freezable: No

DIRECTIONS

1. Line a pastry tin with the pastry, then add some parchment paper before pouring on some pastry beans or rice on top to blind bake. Select the BAKE function and set to 160 degrees and bake for 25 minutes.
2. Empty out the beans/rice and cover the base with jam.
3. Place the butter, sugar and syrup into the main pot and select the SAUTE function set to MEDIUM heat until it's all melted. Alternatively, it may be microwaved for 2 minutes if preferred.
4. In a separate bowl, add the melted liquid to the cornflakes and stir until covered. Put the mix into the pastry case and BAKE at 160 degrees for 10 minutes.

STICKY TOFFEE PUDDING

Prep Time - 10/12m	Cook Time - 40m	Serves - 2	Vegetarian ✓

INGREDIENTS

For the toffee sauce:

90g butter/margarine

90 light brown sugar

250ml double cream

For the pudding:

100g light brown sugar

112g self raising-flour

38g butter/margarine

1 egg

1 tbsp golden syrup

100g dates without the pips

½ tsp bicarbonate of soda

Hot water

Difficulty: Easy/Medium

Ninja® Functions: BAKE, SAUTE

Freezable: Yes

DIRECTIONS

1. Add the dates to the main pot, and then enough hot water to cover them. Add the bicarbonate of soda and stir. Leave for 5 minutes.
2. Blend together the flour, butter, sugar, and dates with the water, egg and golden syrup. Place baking paper into a 3" loaf tin and grease. Add the batter, place it on the low rack in the main pot and select BAKE function set to 150 degrees and bake for 30 minutes. Remove the cake from the machine. Wash the main pot.
3. For the toffee sauce, add the sugar, butter and cream to the man pot and select SAUTE set at LOW, heat up the mixture and keep stirring until it has thickened.
4. Slice the pudding and pour the toffee sauce over it and enjoy!

KEY LIME PIE

Prep Time - 40m	Cook Time - 13m	Serves - 6/8	Vegetarian ✓

INGREDIENTS

83g butter

1 tbsp honey

1 pack of ginger biscuits (crumbed)

4 limes (zest and juice)

1 tbsp icing sugar

300ml double cream

397g condensed milk

3 egg yolks

Difficulty: Medium

Ninja® Functions: SAUTE, BAKE

Freezable: No

DIRECTIONS

1. Add the butter to the main pot together with melted butter and select the SAUTE function set at MEDIUM. Once melted add in the crumbed biscuits, then add the honey and stir until they are covered in the melted butter.

2. Take the biscuit mix and press it into a 7x3" baking tin, squashing it to the sides and bottom, and put in the fridge for 30 minutes to chill.

3. Mix the condensed milk, zest of 3 limes, as well as the juice with 3 egg yolks. Pour into the tin over the biscuit base. Select the BAKE function set at 140 degrees and bake for 13 minutes. Once complete, leave to cool for 20 minutes. Push the pie out of the mould onto a plate.

4. Mix/whisk the cream until it turns stiff. Mix in the zest of the remaining lime, keeping a little aside, then the lime juice and icing sugar.

5. Carefully put the icing on the key lime pie using a fork to make lines and to flatten, then sprinkle the last of the lime zest on top.

DORSET APPLE CAKE

Prep Time - 10/15	Cook Time - 45m	Serves - 6	Vegetarian ✓

INGREDIENTS
115g unsalted butter, diced and chilled
225g self-raising flour
2 tsp ground cinnamon
115g light brown sugar
1 large egg, beaten
Approx. 7 tbsp milk
225g Bramley apples, peeled, cored and diced
100g sultanas
2 tbsp demerara sugar

Difficulty: Medium
Ninja® Functions: BAKE
Freezable: No

DIRECTIONS

1. Select the BAKE function on the machine and preheat the to 160 degrees. Grease and line a deep cake tin that fits the machine, with baking parchment.

2. Mix the flour and cinnamon together in a large bowl. Add the butter and rub into the flour using your fingertips, until it resembles fine breadcrumbs. Stir in the light brown sugar. Beat in the egg followed by approximately 7 tbsp of milk – add it gradually until a smooth, thick batter is formed.

3. Add the apples and sultanas and mix to combine. Scrape the batter into the prepared tin and gently level out. Sprinkle over the demerara sugar and BAKE for 45 minutes at 160 degrees until golden, and a skewer inserted into the middle comes out clean. Keep checking with a temperature probe if you have one. You are looking for about 90°C in the centre.

4. Allow to cool in the tin for 15 minutes and then carefully turn out onto a wire rack to cool further.

HONEY CAKE

Prep Time - 15	Cook Time - 40m	Serves - 8	Vegetarian ✓

INGREDIENTS
240g plain flour
1 teaspoon baking powder
Pinch of salt
¼ tsp ground cinnamon
¼ tsp baking soda
227g unsalted softened butter
110g light brown sugar
80ml honey plus extra for garnishing
4 eggs
1 tsp vanilla extract
30g almonds sliced

Difficulty: Medium
Ninja® Functions: BAKE
Freezable: No

DIRECTIONS

1. In a bowl, mix together the dry ingredients leaving the almonds separate.
2. Add the butter, honey, eggs and vanilla extract and mix well.
3. Using an 8" baking tin, lined with parchment, pour in the mixture.
4. BAKE on 150 degrees for 40 minutes adding the almonds after 20m. Check with a cake stick that its cooked right through before removing.
5. Leave to cool and drizzle some honey before serving.

Smoothies/Shakes

STRAWBERRY SMOOTHIE

Prep Time - 5m	Blend Time - Auto IQ	Serves - 3 Small	Vegetarian ✔	Gluten Free ✔

INGREDIENTS

1 x punnet of strawberries
½ x punnet of blueberries
1 tbsp honey
1 cup almond milk
1 cup plain natural yoghurt
Water if required

Difficulty: Easy
Ninja® Functions: AUTO IQ
Freezable: Yes

DIRECTIONS

1. Add the above ingredients to the blender jug.
2. Fill to around an inch below the top with water, if needed.
3. BLEND and serve.

SUMMER SUNSHINE SMOOTHIE

Prep Time - 5m	Blend Time - Auto IQ	Serves - 3 Small	Vegetarian ✔	Gluten Free ✔

INGREDIENTS

1 apple (peeled, quartered and de-seeded)
1 pear (peeled, cut the same size as the apple, de-seeded)
1 orange (peeled and segmented)
A handful of pineapple pieces (peeled and chopped)
Cover with water

Difficulty: Easy
Ninja® Functions: AUTO IQ
Freezable: Yes

DIRECTIONS

1. Add the above ingredients to the blender jug.
2. Top up with water so there's around an inch left from the top. BLEND, then if using, add ice cubes for a refreshing, cold, summer drink.
3. Serve.

DOUBLE CHOCOLATE MILKSHAKE

Prep Time - 5m	Blend Time - 20/30	Serves – 1 to 2	Vegetarian ✔	Gluten Free ✔

INGREDIENTS

200ml milk semi-skimmed

4 scoops of chocolate ice cream GF – Please check for 'may contain' ingredient advisories.

1 tbsp chocolate sauce GF – Please check for 'may contain' ingredient advisories.

Squirty cream to top

Difficulty: Easy

Ninja® Functions: MAX BLEND

Freezable: No

DIRECTIONS

1. Add the above ingredients and BLEND for around 20-30 seconds.
2. Pour into one large or two small glasses.
3. Complete your shake with your topping of choice - mine's cream!
4. Serve.

CRANBERRY, AVOCADO AND CHERRY SMOOTHIE

Prep Time - 2/3m	Blend Time - Auto IQ	Serves - 3 Small	Vegetarian ✔	Gluten Free ✔

INGREDIENTS
1 cup frozen cranberries
1 avocado (destoned, skin removed)
Heaped handful frozen cherries
Cranberry juice

Difficulty: Easy
Ninja® Functions: AUTO IQ
Freezable: Yes

DIRECTIONS

1. Add cherries to halfway up in the blender jug.
2. Add all other ingredients, filling to one inch from the top with the cranberry juice and BLEND.
3. Pour the mixture into 3 small glasses. Serve.

STRAWBERRY AND BANANA ZING SMOOTHIE

Prep Time - 2/3m	Blend Time - Auto IQ	Serves - 3 Small	Vegetarian ✓	Gluten Free ✓

INGREDIENTS
1 banana
8 large strawberries
3 tbsp frozen Greek yoghurt
250ml pure orange juice or more if needed

Difficulty: Easy
Ninja® Functions: AUTO IQ
Freezable: Yes

DIRECTIONS

1. Add the above ingredients to the blender jug and BLEND.
2. Pour into 2 small glasses.
3. Serve.

SMOOTHIE WITH AN INDIAN TWIST

Prep Time - 2m	Blend Time - Auto IQ	Serves - 2	Vegetarian ✔

INGREDIENTS
4 strawberries
6 raspberries
6 blackberries
1 satsuma
1 banana
250ml cold water leaving space for it to mix.
½ a teaspoon Shan® fruit chaat mix

Difficulty: Easy
Ninja® Functions: SMOOTHIE
Freezable: Yes

DIRECTIONS

1. Add the above ingredients to the jug and select the SMOOTHIE function.
2. Pour into 2 glasses.
3. Serve.

FRUITY BREAKFAST SMOOTHIE WITH A FOOD ART TWIST

Prep Time - 2/3m	Blend Time - Auto IQ	Serves - 2	Vegetarian ✔	Gluten Free ✔

INGREDIENTS
1 banana
A handful of blueberries, raspberries, grapes (selection up to you)
1 satsuma
250ml cold water leaving space at the top

Difficulty: Easy
Ninja® Functions: SMOOTHIE
Freezable: Yes

DIRECTIONS

1. Add the above ingredients to the jug and select the SMOOTHIE function.
2. Pour into 2 glasses.
3. Serve.

CHOCOLATE ORANGE AND CARAMEL MILKSHAKE

| Prep Time - 2/3m | Blend Time - Max Blend | Serves - 1 | Vegetarian ✔ | Gluten Free✔ |

INGREDIENTS

150ml milk

2 big scoops of caramel and vanilla ice cream GF
– Please check for 'may contain' ingredient advisories.

Half a bag of dairy milk giant orange buttons

1tbsp chocolate sauce

Difficulty: Easy

Ninja® Functions: MAX BLEND

Freezable: No

DIRECTIONS

1. MAX BLEND the above ingredients.
2. Stop it when the countdown gets to 20 seconds for a thicker milkshake with bits or keep going for a smoother milkshake.

PEANUT BUTTER AND BANANA SMOOTHIE

Prep Time - 2/3m	Blend Time - Max Blend	Serves - 1	Vegetarian ✔	Gluten Free ✔

INGREDIENTS
2 bananas
4 tbsp yoghurt
4 tbsp peanut butter GF – Please check for
'may contain' ingredient advisories.
250ml pure orange juice

Difficulty: Easy
Ninja® Functions: MAX BLEND
Freezable: No

DIRECTIONS

1. MAX BLEND the above ingredients for around 20 seconds, then serve.

MANGO AND SEED SMOOTHIE

Prep Time - 2/3m	Blend Time – Auto IQ	Serves - 2	Vegetarian ✓

INGREDIENTS

Small handful of mango, pineapple and grapefruit pieces
1 banana
3 tbsp natural yoghurt
300ml mango juice
Top with chia and linseeds

Difficulty: Easy
Ninja® Functions: MAX BLEND
Freezable: No

DIRECTIONS

1. Add the above fruit and yogurt to the blender, top with mango juice to fill to the max fill line and blend on AUTO IQ until its finished.
2. Now sprinkle with chia and linseeds,
3. serve

Dehydrate

DEHYDRATED TOMATOES

Prep Time - 5/8m	Dehydrate - 7hrs	Serves - Batch	Vegan✔	Gluten Free✔

INGREDIENTS
Punnet of vine tomatoes
1 tsp powdered garlic
1 tsp mixed herbs
Pinch of salt
1 tbsp olive oil
2 cloves of garlic (sliced)

Difficulty: Easy
Ninja® Functions: DEHYDRATE
Freezable: No

DIRECTIONS

1. Spray or toss the tomatoes in olive oil. Sprinkle on the garlic powder, mixed herbs and salt. Place the tomatoes on the dehydration tray and select the DEHYDRATE function set to 70 degrees for 7 hours.
2. Store in olive oil in a jar with some fresh garlic cloves.
3. This keeps well in a cool dark cupboard for a couple of months.

DEHYDRATED HERBS

| Prep Time - 5m | Dehydrate – 5hrs | Serves - Batch | Vegan✔ | Gluten Free✔ |

INGREDIENTS

I used thyme and basil, fresh from the garden, but you can buy these from many greengrocers and supermarkets. It can make a large quantity, so I'd say 2 to 3 bags of each.

Difficulty: Easy
Ninja® Functions: DEHYDRATE
Freezable: No

DIRECTIONS

1. Remove the herbs, leaving the stems out.
2. Add the herbs on top of the insert tray.
3. Set to dehydrate for 5 hours at 60°C.
   (The fan does blow the herbs around, so make sure your pan is cleaned well afterwards.)

   Store in an airtight jar. The flavour is amazing!

DEHYDRATED APPLE, ORANGE AND BANANA

Prep Time – 8m	Dehydrate - 9hrs	Serves - Batch	Vegan✔️	Gluten Free✔️

INGREDIENTS

1 apple
1 banana
1 orange
Baking parchment

Tips/Variations (optional):
Store in an airtight container in a cool dark place - can last 6 months if stored correctly. They must be completely dehydrated to do this, check for any moisture before storing. Dehydrate for longer if necessary.

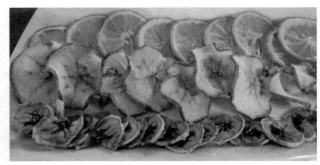

Difficulty: Easy
Ninja® Functions: DEHYDRATE
Freezable: No

DIRECTIONS

1. Slice the fruit very thin (no bigger than 2mm if possible) and arrange on the baking parchment on the dehydration racks (cut it to fit to size as required.
2. Carefully place the racks into the main pot. Select the DEHYDRATE function set to 60 degrees for 9 hours.
3. Storage - keep in an air-tight jar or container until ready to use.

DEHYDRATED VASE DECORATIONS

Prep Time - 5/8m	Dehydrate – 9hrs	Serves - Batch	Vegan✔	Gluten Free✔

INGREDIENTS
1 orange
1 lime
1 lemon

For decoration:
Festive bells
Cinnamon sticks
Fairy lights

Difficulty: Easy
Ninja® Functions: DEHYDRATE
Freezable: No

DIRECTIONS

1. Thinly slice the fruit and arrange it on the dehydrate racks.
2. Carefully place the racks into the main pot of the machine.
3. Select the DEHYDRATE function and set to 60 degrees for 8 to 9 hours.
4. Enjoy!

DEHYDRATED DOOR WREATH

Prep Time - 5/8m	Dehydrate – 10hrs	Serves - Batch	Vegan✔	Gluten Free✔

INGREDIENTS
1 orange
1 lemon
Festive pinecones, baubles, cinnamon and some fairy lights for decoration

Difficulty: Easy
Ninja® Functions: DEHYDRATE
Freezable: No

DIRECTIONS

1. Slice the orange and lemon and arrange on the dehydration rack.
2. Carefully place the rack into the main pot of the machine.
3. Select the DEHYDRATE function and set to 60 degrees for around 9 to 10 hours.
4. Add to a homemade, or a shop bought wreath with cinnamon, pinecones and any other decorations using glue and string to attach.

DEHYDRATED MUSHROOMS

Prep Time – 5/8m	Dehydrate – 8hrs	Serves - Batch	Vegan✔	Gluten Free✔

INGREDIENTS
Thinly sliced mushrooms around 3mm
thick. As many as you can fit on your
rack/racks
Lightly spray olive oil
Sprinkle with some dried herbs of your
choice, here's some ideas, nice with dry or
some fresh:
Dried mixed herbs
Smoked paprika
Garlic and basil
BBQ flavouring
Chilli
Soy sauce brushed on
Oregano
Thyme
Rosemary

Difficulty: Easy
Ninja® Functions: DEHYDRATE
Freezable: No

Tips/Variations (optional):
Store in an airtight container in a cool dark
place, these were used within 6 months but
they can last over a year if stored correctly.

DIRECTIONS

1. Slice the mushrooms as thinly as possible and lay out, spray lightly with some olive oil and add some flavourings of your choice, I made three different flavours in this batch, or you can flavour with just one, there's some ideas above but you can create your own. Alternatively, you can just dehydrate with no flavouring.

INDEX

- GF ** - Can be adapted to Gluten Free by swapping the highlighted ingredients to GF

- GF - Naturally Gluten free recipes do not require ingredients substitution as they are gluten free as listed.

- VE – Suitable for Vegans

- V – Suitable for Vegetarians

Printed in Great Britain
by Amazon

37546669R00066